To: Shelly — *Paul Freda*

THE TYRANNY OF UNCONDITIONAL LOVE
WHEN LOGICAL LOVING LIMITS FAIL.

Effective and accurate parenting for your problem child

PAUL DOMINIC FREDA, M.D.

Copyright © 2012 Paul Dominic Freda, M.D.
All rights reserved.
ISBN: 1475132778
ISBN 13: 9781475132779

CONTENTS

Preface v

Chapter 1 The Victim 1

Chapter 2 Love Imbalance versus Chemical Imbalance 9

Chapter 3 Unconditional Love 17

Chapter 4 The Escape Clause 25

Chapter 5 Why Your Parenting Strategies Don't Work 41

Chapter 6 Mental Illness 49

Chapter 7 Eliminating the Escape Clause 67

Chapter 8 Suspending Your Love 85

Chapter 9 It's Nonnegotiable 91

Chapter 10 Don't Just Do Something. Observe 99

Chapter 11 Act Your Age? 121

Summary 134

PREFACE

I became board-certified in psychiatry over thirty years ago and have practiced in the private and public sectors for almost as long. I have treated thousands of patients, from three to ninety-three ("womb to tomb"), and have continued to use psychodynamically oriented therapy for individuals, couples, families, and groups.

I've seen many changes in the practice of psychiatry. A fabulously persisting explosion in the field of psychiatric medications is occurring, allowing psychiatrists to deconstruct mental illnesses into their component parts, thereby more effectively targeting specific symptoms without causing unwanted side effects. While this is undoubtedly a wonderful thing, many psychiatrists have found themselves to be little more than pill-pushers, lacking both the time and energy to do much more than monitor a patient's response to medications. But through the years, I have continued to make use of my training in psychodynamics in order to do more than merely medicate. Old-school theories, such as those of Freud, Jung, and Erikson, continue to have their place in helping a person, a couple, or a family live a happier life.

But along with the vast increases in the knowledge of how our brains work—which allows more precise pharmacological treatment of mental illnesses—there is also the continuing trend of *medicalizing* more and more types of problem behaviors. Viewing, say, violence as a problem behavior due to a brain abnormality is good in the sense that we know more about it, but it's bad in the sense that we might let some criminals off the hook.

Another trend in the disciplines of psychiatry, social work, and the judicial system as well—and what finally prompted me to write this book—is the continual viewing of our children's problem behaviors in the same way: blaming some genetic flaw for, say, autism or some prior trauma for a child's oppositional, defiant, or aggressive behaviors.

And there has been a troubling trend in our society, especially during the last two decades, in which parents are being disempowered and children are being emboldened. This is particularly troublesome because most parents—at least the ones desperate enough to come to me—are not even aware of it. Though they suspect it's not the natural order of things, they've no idea how their children got so out of control—their family's lives turned upside down. These parents feel powerless in their own homes. Many parents are terrified of their own children, afraid of being verbally abused, physically attacked, or reported to social services on false (or founded) allegations. Suddenly, parents are at the mercy of their own children, children who, let's face it, can be merciless.

Over the past several years, I've found myself making the same suggestions or recommendations to hundreds of parents, hoping to create an awareness that their situations are not necessary, not normal, and are completely backwards. I've offered the same strategies designed to help them wrest control over their households, re-empower themselves, appropriately discipline their children, and stop being afraid of their children. It got to the point where many parents asked me if I'd written a book about this. Well, here goes.

Before we get started, most parents referred to in this book are female, either biological, foster, or adoptive mothers, because even after half a century of heightened awareness, our society persists with the woman as the emotional hub of the family. In addition, the male parental role model usually finds my approach more reasonable than the female parental role model, largely because females are bred to allow and endure, while males are taught to love tough and not enable. My approach, as written in this book, is not fluffy, not warm-fuzzy, and not yielding, making it difficult for many parents to even consider what they are about to read. Keep in mind that this approach is not necessary— or even appropriate—for the majority of troubled children and adolescents. Rather, it is intended for the parents who have tried logic and limits and love—but who continue misinterpreting their role as parent. It's time for the "business of parenting" to be seriously addressed—perhaps utilizing sessions exclusively for parents, because quite often it is they, more than their children, who need the help.

I hope I've referred to the children using fairly evenly divided genders. Significant gender differences in occurrences of behavior or attitude problems will be mentioned, and several distinct childhood mental illnesses will be described as needed. Vignettes (with confidentiality preserved) from decades of work—and many successes!—with frustrated children and parents are interwoven throughout the text.

Finally, this book will address the issue of nature versus nurture and heredity versus environment. How sick must a person be to get away with bad behavior? Is it the ADD or is it willful disobedience? Is your child unable to reasonably cooperate with you or just unwilling to? As you might suspect, it's possible—and correct—to discipline your child and still empathize with his or her mental illness.

Let's begin.

Paul Dominic Freda, M.D.
October 2012

CHAPTER 1

THE VICTIM

You've read the books. You've attended the lectures and the parenting classes. Family therapy addresses the love your child needs and the limits you must logically set. You know you love your child. And you still like and enjoy your child, don't you?

But you're here in the principal's office with Joey, your fourteen-year-old son, who applied Ben-gay to an older student's jockstrap. Retaliating to an in-school suspension, he hoarded lunch meat for two weeks so that it would spoil, and then he slipped it into the lunch pot. Half the school is thinner now. He flaunts his defiance at authority and bullies younger kids. He targets others with arrogant ridicule and disrespect.

And Joey shows no remorse.

The latest event—which triggered your current visit to the principal's office—involved Joey's attacking another student, wrestling him to the ground, choking him until he was unconscious, and then preparing to jam a pencil into the boy's eye... when a teacher happened to turn a corner at just the right time and (with great effort, you're told) pulled Joey off the other boy. The teacher claims Joey then tried to drive the pencil into *her* eye.

It took another teacher, the high school football coach, and the PE instructor to wrestle Joey off her, during which he grabbed her crotch and severely bruised her. The police were called; Joey is on his way to jail again, claiming that *he* was assaulted by the other student and sexually molested by the female teacher. After your bailing him out last night, not only does Joey not show remorse, but he is also furious about what he alleges happened *to him!* Despite four adult witnesses who share the same account of what happened, Joey denies his behavior, insists he is innocent of any wrongdoing, and now accuses others of victimizing him.

Wait a minute. Doesn't Joey behave like this at home? When he was eleven, it took a while to figure out why the cat was throwing up, your petty cash was disappearing, and the right half of your daughter's head was getting bald spots. More recently, you've had to hide the marks Joey's left on you, fearing that others would suspect your spouse of being abusive. No matter what you do, you can't elicit an ounce of remorse from him, and he quickly turns things around so that he feels victimized. Hmmm.

Not only has Joey become a persistent irritant to you, your spouse, and Joey's six-year-old sister, but your irritation has actually grown to fear and dread. This is not the first time you've bailed Joey out of jail. Two years ago, he ran away from home at midnight, broke into the neighbor's house, and drank their liquor. Last year he was arrested for stalking a girl in his class—something you had a hard time believing. You do recall taking his side and making up an alibi for him, don't you? This child who once brought you joy and fulfillment now brings annoyance, fear, and apprehension. You are afraid of your own son. Does this ring true with you? Did you bail him out this time out of love or because you dreaded what he'd do if you let him spend a night or two in jail?

Now, in Principal Brown's office, you're very uneasy with the latest allegations. (This is on top of a difficult day at work and getting a flat on your way to the school.) You're tired, and you're angry that you're here. And what got you here? Joey's alleged behavior, or the school again demanding your response to yet another crisis? Whose fault is it, really? It would be easy to blame the school. How did Joey have access to the jockstrap and the school kitchen anyway? Don't they monitor children here? Kids get into squabbles all the time. Did he really try to enucleate someone's eye? If so, something must've really made him mad.

Mr. Brown clears his throat. He's uncomfortable. "Mrs. Enableson, you know the facts as we see them. This is not the first time our school community has suffered. Joey continues victimizing other children, and the school community is at risk." He shifts in his seat. "Joey's been suspended eight times this year." Throwing up his hands, he adds, "We have no choice but to expel him."

Joey squirms, his face showing angry resentment. Although Joey *seems* distraught at Mr. Brown's report, you sense his boredom; you sense he really couldn't care less. But on the other hand, Joey could be feeling sad. Maybe your son's apparent ennui is really the school's fault. You're feeling uneasy, and it's not the first time you've felt this way in the principal's office.

Whose side are you on? There *are* many sides to this story, right?

Now, I assume you've found yourself in a similar position, wondering whose fault it really is. Your child is once again "in trouble." The principal wants you to know what he knows about Joey. But does he know what *you* know about your son? Can you come clean right now, in the principal's office? Or is Joey the victim here?

Yes, your son's in trouble with the school. But isn't he in trouble with you and your spouse also? Is Joey even thinking of what he puts the family through at home, while squirming before you in the principal's office, a purely petulant puss right now? You sense his complete lack of remorse, his lack of sadness. He doesn't care about what he did, doesn't care about being called into the office, and doesn't regret your being called into the school today. Not only that, but you also sense that he's angry about this whole situation. And your discomfort *here* will be eclipsed by the hell Joey will put you through once you get back home. You know he'll make you pay for anything less than sticking up for him and finding fault with the school. Joey wants you to feel sorry for him, to see him as the true victim here.

Guess what? Joey *is* the victim here. But he's not the victim of the school, and he's not the victim of bad genes. Unfortunately, he is like many other children needing psychiatric help, whose parents wonder what is truly wrong with them. Does your constantly irritated Megan persistently defy you, blame others for unmet wants, verbally and emotionally abuse the family, and throw temper fits at the slightest frustrations? Does your belligerent Tucker slam doors, punch walls, taunt the family pets, cut on himself, and hit, bite, or kick you and his siblings? Has your child "always been this way" but was never considered a problem until first grade?

Guess what? Megan has oppositional defiant disorder (ODD), and Tucker has conduct disorder (CD), both of which are mental illnesses distinct from attention deficit disorder (ADD) and bipolar disorder. For you, this means Megan and Tucker weren't born with their problems. They were **bred** into them. Our pal Joey is not the victim of an inherited bipolar disorder, a schizophrenic psychosis, an autism gene, or ADD. Rather, he is the victim of exaggerated, overemphasized, and overabundant love. Put simply, he is the victim of this crazy obsession we have with unconditional love. You hear it all the time: "I love him unconditionally!" "I love him to death!" "Of course I love my child!"

Now, is unconditional love working for you?

Probably not.

Do you want to continue shoving that stick into the ground, keep bringing it up, and keep insisting on it? You prefer to think that your child is out of your control because of a chemical imbalance causing him or her to defy you—and that heaping unconditional love will convince him or her to change.

Why do you prefer to think this way? For what purpose? To benefit whom? Your child—or you? Most parents I've interviewed actually succumb to this insanity to avoid feeling guilty. They insist on unconditionally loving their child for their OWN benefit—not their child's. And it's obvious that it's not for their child's benefit, because they're bringing their child in to see *me*.

So let's get real. (1) your son is out of control because you're loving him too much; (2) your daughter is out of control because

The Tyranny of Unconditional Love

you're loving her unconditionally; (3) unconditional love is not good for your son or your daughter; and (4) unconditional love is the current obsession, vital for infants and toddlers, but a recipe for disaster after that.

And if you're hot about drugs—psychotropic intervention or psychiatric drugs—*please!* You are among dozens of parents who have come to me insisting that their child needs drugs. With no exception, the parent makes it clear: "Doc, I've spoiled my son for six years. Now fix him with Ritalin."

Ritalin fixes ADD.
Abilify stabilizes bipolarity.
Conditional love fixes the rest.

That's it. Read on for the explanations.

CHAPTER 2

LOVE IMBALANCE VERSUS CHEMICAL IMBALANCE

So what made Joey do those things at home and at school? Are you tempted, like many parents, to view your child's willful, provocative behaviors as acts not only beyond your control but also beyond her or his control? Would it feel better to attribute the cause of Joey's behavior—rude, arrogant, and obnoxious as it is—to some genetic flaw? Would you rather medicalize his attitude and behaviors—strikingly defiant and spiteful as they are—into mitigated demeanor and unintentional conduct completely out of his control? If you've gotten beyond genetics and diseases, and if you've already accepted your child's behavior as a product of your relationship with him or her, have all the love and logic and limits failed to help?

I assume you're thinking, *I've tried everything. Nothing seems to work. Nothing matters to him.* Assuming this is true, I will explain what it is you need to do.

> If you're willing to accept the fact that you're doing something wrong—insisting on limitless, unconditional love, which is proving illogical—then continue reading.
> And if you can accept the fact that you have *not* tried everything, try this:
> ***Logically limited, conditional love.***

Let's examine a typical child/adolescent psychiatric interview. A parent, usually the mom, brings her child—anywhere from four to sixteen years old—in to see me, often speculating that her child has attention deficit disorder (ADD) or bipolar disorder. She asks for medication to help diminish and stop her child's oppositional and defiant attitude or hostile, violent conduct behavior problems.

I would explain that attention deficit hyperactivity disorder (ADHD) behaviors are typically not deliberate, not hostile, not premeditated, not targeted, and not spiteful as a response to unmet wants. *They usually do not occur in the family system context of a power struggle.* (Think of a Superball thrown against a wall: it doesn't care what it strikes next; it's random. These random, impulsive behaviors represent the "h" in "hyperactivity," the hyperactive child feeling enormous pressure to *act* on the random, nonprioritized thoughts that torment the ADD child.) Quite often, the mom is too tormented and pressured herself to stop and wonder whether her child's behaviors represent a family process or not. She has great difficulty listening to the distinction between targeted and nontargeted behaviors, insisting that I prescribe Ritalin for any behaviors that *are* deliberate, hostile, premeditated, targeted, and spiteful. Not only would Ritalin not help, but it could also make the behaviors worse; it would distract from the child's taking ownership of some behaviors, and the mother would likely still have a monster on her hands even after Ritalin calmed the true overactivity.

I would also address the true nature of bipolar disorder. If you say your child has mood swings, does this mean your child is bipolar? Ah, that depends on how you define this overused term. Nowadays, bipolar disorder is so popular that it makes you wonder, is there anyone who is *not* bipolar? Who among us does *not* have mood swings—if you are interpreting this crucial feature of bipolarity in its literal sense? If you've spent twenty minutes on hold with your physician's office, trying to schedule a lab test, and then you have to press 1 if it's a CT scan, press 2 if it involves dye, and then press 3 if…and suddenly your call is lost, wouldn't your mood "swing" at that moment? Unfortunately, peevish pity-pot parties do not capture the true emotional swings necessary for a diagnosis of bipolar disorder.

Although both ADD and bipolar disorder are understood as chemical imbalances eluding the Goldilocks-perfect soup of neurotransmitters in our brains, correcting that imbalance with psychotropics won't necessarily correct the other issue. Even *with* medications, your child may continue with resentful attitudes and caustic behaviors that override that perfect chemical balance.

Many years ago, I saw Janice, a thirty-eight-year-old woman diagnosed with bipolar disorder, who was doing fairly well on a combination of Seroquel, Depakote, and Abilify. One day she brought her eleven-year-old son, Jared, to see me for a follow-up after he was discharged from a psychiatric hospital on the exact same meds, he, too, diagnosed with bipolar disorder. His history was full of truancy, curfew violations, vandalism, opposition to rules, defiance of authority, animal cruelty, fire-setting, and a bitter, arrogantly cavalier attitude. He'd been to juvenile detention many times. After three weeks in the hospital, his bipolarity was deemed under control.

But Janice told me that Jared still had a very poor attitude and, with him out of the room, showed me some bruises he'd inflicted on her. When asked if she'd called the police when he physically bullied her, she said, "No! I can't do that to him. I love him. He's my child." She sobbed, and after a bit, she choked out the words, "I caused this anyway. I gave him this disease. If it weren't for me, he wouldn't be bipolar!"

This was an indication that she was stuck giving him unconditional love, not because of her actual love for him—and I'm not implying she doesn't love him—but out of guilt for thinking that his problems were caused by a disease that she gave him. Janice's not calling the police was to placate herself, not just to placate Jared. She wanted to reduce the anxiety of the guilt she'd feel if she had him put in jail for a while. To her credit, she fully understood these dynamics, but she still wanted me to see him, hopefully to increase his medications so that he'd treat her better.

Well, I spent some time with Jared, and to *his* credit, he had some understanding of this issue as well. Did he know he was milking it for all it was worth? Did he know that having bipolar disorder was a free ride for him? Did he realize that the diagnosis—being sick, having a disease—played on his mom's guilt and caused her to overcompensate with unconditional love?

Of course he did. But what, I thought, about the robust medication regimen he was on? He showed no side effects, didn't appear overmedicated…and then it dawned on me that he was actually cheeking his meds and not ingesting them at all. He really wanted his mother to continue believing she had a "sick" child on her hands.

Well. Imagine that. I told Jared to wait outside my office in our waiting room while I resumed my meeting with Janice, touching on these issues in order to see just where her ambivalence about her son lay. We had a nice discussion, which, after a while, was interrupted by commotion in the waiting room.

We opened the door and found Jared sitting on the floor with his back against the front door, cursing, his verbal wrath escalating in volume and cadence. Nerf toys were strewn all about the waiting room. My receptionist was calmly reminding him to place the toys in the box he'd found them in, but he wouldn't comply. He was pounding his feet into the floor—spitting, kicking, cursing—and when we opened my office door and he saw his mom, he escalated even more, making quite a hectic scene. It took me a while to get a word in edgewise, and as he caught his breath, I said, "Jared. You've got five minutes to either put the toys back in the box or not. After five minutes, your chance to comply will end, and you will leave the office." He looked at me, actually growling, calling me colorful epithets. And then I offered, "And y'know what, Jared? Whether you choose to put the toys back or not, we really don't care. You do what you want."

With that, he abruptly got up and began to retrieve the Nerf toys and throw them into the box, but not without growls and curses, anything to make us miserable. Now, as the box filled up, his throwing the toys at the box resulted in their landing in the box and then bouncing back out. It was with carefully hidden smirks that we witnessed his returning all the toys to the box, the last one needing six attempts before he thought to drop it and not throw it in.

At that, I said, "Thank you, Jared." He looked at me in awe. *I had responded to his complying with my request, not to the awful manner in which he went about it.*

I then glanced at Janice and said, "Um, bipolar disorder?"

Now Janice was able to grasp the true nature of the problem—that something *in addition to* Jared's catching the bipolar gene from Mom needed serious attention. In this particular case, Jared's bipolar disorder became, actually, an afterthought. Finding the effective recipe of Depakote, Abilify, and Ritalin (yes, he also has ADD) was my job as a psychopharmacologist; uncovering the reasons why Jared thought he could run roughshod over Mom was my job as a family therapist.

And so, with a child's chemistry corrected, I then explore the history of the parent-child relationship. When did the bad attitude or aggressive behaviors start? Typically, Mom will say, "Oh, he's always been that way," recalling her child being difficult from as early as two years of age. Although Mom has no problem answering that question, very often she has a problem with the next question: when your child started being difficult, how did you handle it? In other words, how did you handle your job as a parent? This is crucial, because it shifts the focus from the child to the parent.

More often than not, Mom responds to this question with some degree of defense, in some cases with umbrage and outrage. She typically reports inability to handle the bad attitude or aggressive behavior. "I've tried everything," she insists, reporting spankings, time-outs, and — this is the favorite — removing toys, video games, iPods, and other items. She also reports that none of these maneuvers seems to bother or in any way affect her child. "He just doesn't care," she sobs.

On the other hand, less often than not, the introspective, astute mom admits that she simply avoided the job of parenting and that her own childhood experience interfered with her taking on the difficult task of parenting her own child. She admits that she allowed herself to become disempowered and that she allowed her child to do and have whatever he or she wanted. Alas, she will admit that she's grown a monster. This mom will also ask for medication — Ritalin for ADD, or perhaps *some*thing for bipolar disorder — but will also see the need for parenting classes and help with her own childhood memories and possible PTSD issues.

Whether you're the mom who refuses to have her role in this scrutinized or the mom who does not deny the part she played, both of these parents avoided the task of parenting their children. Thus, identifying the true task of parenting and figuring out how to do it is the focus of this book.

Human offspring depend on their parents long after other animals release their kids into the world. We tend to perceive the time our children are dependent on us as the amount of time needed to ensure they are *ready for* the world. We seldom perceive this time as the amount required to make them *tolerable to* the world.

Imagine a tiger teaching her cub *not* to be ready for the survival-of-the-fittest ways of our world or allowing her cub to grow up thinking he doesn't have to defend himself or doesn't have to hunt in order to eat. And yet we have parents who allow their children to grow up thinking they are fit for the world when they aren't. Fortunately, the tiger cub has its instinct to rely on, so his world-readiness is inherent. But with humans, world-readiness is beyond basic survival fight-or-flight imperatives, and this fact is not something to be taken for granted. In order to be ready for the world, our children must be, among other things, *taught* how to be *tolerable* to this world.

My job as a psychiatrist is not just to throw pills at the child, but also to address the problem in her or his environment — the shift in power from parent to child. Whether the child has ODD (more often in daughters) or CD (more often in sons), the parents have lost their leverage. *The imbalance is not within the child's brain; it is within the parent-child relationship.*

CHAPTER 3

UNCONDITIONAL LOVE

AT THE RISK of sounding glib, Joey does what he does because he *can*. Like the boy who owns all the marbles, if *he* leaves, there's no game. So you do anything to make sure he hangs around. This guy can change the rules, he can cheat, or whatever, because he owns the marbles. Just as he holds all the marbles, Joey holds all the options. He has no external reason to cooperate by supplying marbles or help or gratitude. To him, life is boring, because he has nothing challenging him and nothing else to strive for. No matter what, he'll still get to keep doing outrageous things. The boy with all the marbles knows he holds enormous power and that he can say or do anything he wants and still have all the marbles. If *you* won the Powerball, would you then be able to tell your boss what you really think? What really keeps *you* from behaving as if you have all the power?

What keeps you from telling your boss to shove it is his *leverage* over you. If you remove that leverage, what, really, does your boss have that would keep you from doing or saying whatever you want to do or say?

If Joey has all the power, he *can* do what he does. If you win sixty million dollars, you can do whatever you want. Both Joey and you would have the intoxicating assurance, he that his parents have no leverage over him and you that your boss has no leverage over you.

And it's leverage that all the self-help books are trying to help you reclaim. These books want you to make a difference in your child's life, to matter to her, to make her understand that you have something important to bring to her.

Leverage

From a pragmatic point of view, leverage is the missing ingredient. Leverage would give Joey or you pause—would stop you in your tracks—before he flips his dad off or you tell your boss his real IQ. If this is beginning to sound cold to you or void of emotion, like a class in accounting or economics, you're getting the point. There's no good or bad here, no righteous justice or harsh injustice. No one (not Joey, not you, not your boss) is good, bad, immoral, or selfish. **We are all opportunists in the economics of interpersonal life.** If I can get away with a shortcut, if I can manipulate you by simply maneuvering to get my way, I will do exactly that—unless there is some leverage making me think twice about doing it.

Your child has a bad attitude and does bad things because he *can*.

Encouraging a better attitude and better behavior is simply not working because you really *don't* have leverage.

Leverage is the only thing that will stop giving your child permission to misbehave.

The Tyranny of Unconditional Love

I encourage you to grasp this essential fact: no matter what you've tried, no matter what you're doing, you are *still* giving your child *permission* to defy you. You still do *not* have the leverage you need in order for him to respect you. You continue avoiding the one thing that, after logical limit-setting and tough love have obviously failed, will at last deter your child from his disruptive/aggressive behaviors or her oppositional/defiant attitudes.

We know these other techniques and strategies don't work, because he continues being out of your control. Therefore, they do not constitute leverage. And that's the thing your child knows beyond a shadow of a doubt: *your heart will eventually make you yield to him.* What I'm telling you is this: In order to wrench this thing around, we need to consider the *business* of parenting.

Simply put, your child is out of control because you love him too much. You care too much, thereby making it unnecessary for *him* to care. In any relationship, caring is mutual. There is a balance that moves back and forth. Of course, with a newborn, the balance totally favors the newborn: total unconditional love. (It's got to be; otherwise, you'd kill the kid.) As your child grows up, the gushy, coddling love will continue to be needed; the balance of love and caring is a one-way street toward the child and away from you. But as the child continues growing, it will become increasingly self-defeating—for you and your child—to keep the same balance. You'd like to keep this balance going, unconditionally loving your child. It really is quite beautiful to continue this, because of its implications, most of which are unconscious; they imply that you can continue loving unconditionally without fear of your child exploiting this. Your child will grow up respecting you and heeding your every word, obeying you, and doing what you ask, even when you eventually begin to thwart your child's wishes and frustrate him or her.

Do you know of any child who persistently exhibits unconditional adoration of his parents? Does any child continue buying everything you say after the age of five or six or seven? Does any child continue believing in Santa Claus?

No. And this is largely independent of IQ. No matter how dumb or how smart children actually are, at some point all children begin to lose their innocence. The child starts questioning what you say and questioning what you tell him or her to do or why you deny certain wishes. This questioning is the exact same process as stopping believing in Santa Claus. This is the ending of the Age of Innocence, and it is precisely *this* that you so desperately want to *not* see come to an end. If you could continue loving your child unconditionally—and your child were to allow this by remaining innocent and not questioning you or your motives—wouldn't this be the ideal arrangement? The story of Adam and Eve's fall from grace is about their losing this arrangement: they started to question why God told them not to eat the fruit of that one particular tree. Why that tree? Why *only* that tree? Why not? What could possibly happen? Are you making that up, God? Isn't it really only an arbitrary whim of yours? What could happen that would be so bad if I took just one bite of the apple? God loves us unconditionally, doesn't he? But God got a big surprise. He couldn't create humans having free will and innocence at the same time. With free will came an inquiring mind and the ability to doubt authority.

Unconditionally loving your child indefinitely requires your child to unconditionally believe and trust you indefinitely. But for good or for bad, that's not the way the world works. Our lack of infallibility makes it necessary to question each other, which unavoidably leads to the option to oppose and defy. Adam and Eve chose to defy God because they doubted he had real leverage over them. Now, could you blame them? He loved them unconditionally, right? But I think God might have assumed that unconditional love and respect are not mutually contradictory (perhaps he reached his Peter Principle?), because as soon as Eve tasted that forbidden fruit, ooops! God realized too late that, nope, his frontal-lobed, free-willing creatures don't respect him. Well, this must've really struck a chord with our Supreme Being, because Adam and Eve's world sure changed, didn't it? You might say that our Old Testament God ran amok, demanding respect everywhere, and you'd be damned if you didn't respect him.

Nowadays, we wonder why a loving God allows bad things to happen to good people. Well, maybe because he ditched the whole unconditional love experiment when we got kicked out of paradise.

In other words, respect and unconditional love really *are* mutually contradictory.

I beg you to consider this contradiction, given how our brains are wired. Because of our opportunistic bent, in our adult world, there's a fine line between loving unconditionally and being a pushover. As a parent, maintaining unconditional love unconditionally will sabotage your child's emotional, mental, social, and spiritual development. I say this because our brains and our world do not work based on unconditional love, and you will be giving your child the wrong idea of how this world of ours works. The minute you make the mistake of relying on unconditional love, the minute you *show your child* that she can get away with defiance because you *love* her, well, that's the exact moment you've stepped onto the slippery slope of doom. At first it's nice; it's cute; it fits, and it makes sense. You both feel so warm, fuzzy, and good.

I see how parents do this, how they show their child that she can get away with defiance because they unconditionally love her.

Mary brings her eight-year-old son, Cole, to see me and reports that Cole tortures the cat, throws dishes when asked to help after dinner, punches holes in walls, and has destroyed five sets of his bedroom door hinges. The thing is, though, while telling me these things with Cole present in the room, she alternates looking at me with looking at him. You've seen that gaze, and you do it yourself. As if she needs his visage to jog her memory, she spends most of her time reporting his outrageous behavior while beholding him and looking at him, with some sort of half-smile on her face. Sometimes her smile is enhanced with a soft chuckle. My outrage at this is tempered only slightly by my understanding that her smile and chuckle might be driven by nerves... because whatever her conscious emotion is, she is *subconsciously* conveying to Cole that she is *pleased*. (We do agree that smiles are subconsciously triggered knee-jerk responses to events that delight us or at least jibe with our personal preferences.) That smile, that chuckle, that pleasant expression—none of it is lost on Cole. In fact, in the complexity of his relationship with his mom, he's counting on it. And in the complexity of the mom-son-shrink relationship, he knows whose "side" she's really on. Her words list her complaints about things she's seeking help to change, but her demeanor shows her love—her unconditional love—toward her son, who then uses this to avoid making changes suggested to them during the course of therapy.

Debra is in the waiting room with her cross, oppositional, defiant five-year-old daughter, Megan, who is busy taunting a toddler and creating commotion. Debra is conversing with another client, and when the commotion distracts her, she turns and yells to Megan, "Stop it! Stop that now." Megan stops. Debra turns back around to continue her conversation. Megan waits a beat or two, notes Mom's inattention to her antics, and then resumes her taunts. Debra's entire demeanor communicates several things: (1) I'm not really interested in your taunting the toddler, Megan; (2) I *am* interested in your distracting me from my conversation; (3) I'll show you that my telling you to stop holds little, if any, clout; (4) go back to what you were doing so that I get distracted again and repeat my directive; (5) and, by the way, Megan, let's continue this dance because it provides me with job security. You'll always need me, your mother, to redirect you and keep you in line. (In other words, I want you to stay immature. Not only do I love you in spite of your immaturity, but I actually *need* you to continue it.)

Bob brings his fourteen-year-old son, Devon, to see me after Devon's school refused to let him return unless a note from me proclaims him not a danger to other students. Devon, like our friend Joey, is holding the school hostage with his bullying of students in lower grades. I recognize that both Devon and Bob are pretty pissed about this mandated referral. Devon blames other students for his bullying them; Bob blames the school system for not "getting over it." They disregard my pointing out that authorities can't just get over his son's "playfully" clicking on the empty chamber of a revolver while pointing it inches away from a girl's face, or that doing something like that will get unwanted administrative attention, or that, morality aside, this stuff is taken seriously. No. Instead, they form a solid allegiance against the school, the parents of the other children, and, now, me. As with so many bullies, Devon is subconsciously acting out his father's antisocial desires. And Bob is quick to come to Devon's defense by insisting that he's Devon's father, Devon's his son, and so on, superficially professing undying love for Devon while in fact propagating the hatred for authority that Bob himself was taught.

These are examples of the tyrannical nature of unconditional love.

> Prolonged use of unconditional love will doom you and your child to a power struggle that will get the best of you, will only get worse and worse, and will ultimately defeat you and alienate your child from you.

CHAPTER 4

THE ESCAPE CLAUSE

I AM FAMILIAR WITH the plethora of books devoted to parenting strategies and child discipline. For moderately terrible situations, those theories and techniques may be fine. But again, if you're reading this, I'll bet those other approaches haven't worked. The contracts, the agreements, the strategies—some of them are pretty good. Tough love is hardly something new. Using logic as well as love—that is, using your frontal lobe as well as your heart—makes sense. We could list reasons for your child's misbehavior, some ways to stay ahead of your child's pissy attitude, strategies to avoid your buttons getting pushed, and the issues that matter to your child so that you can agree on a contract between you and her. Sure, you'll learn the reasons why your child or teen is out of control as well as some ideas for crafting a meaningful contract in order to get her back into control. And while you're doing all this reading and all this work, what is your child doing? Is she, too, reading, researching, and doing her part? No, she's not. She's not the least bit interested in the situation—except, of course, to continue the status quo, making your life miserable and having the family tremble on eggshells around her (also known as getting her way).

I've seen many of these situations displayed in the office, the degree of family misery anywhere from mild—with those nervous smiles and chuckles—to profound: Dad is outraged, and Mom is sobbing. They mention various examples of their son's or their daughter's inappropriate behaviors and caustic attitudes. Some phrases I hear are common: "I don't understand why she's angry all the time;" "I've tried everything, but nothing seems to matter to him;" "We argue all the time, about everything, the least little thing." The list usually includes examples of the son's aggression or examples of the daughter's arrogant, haughty attitude. Broken doors, punched walls, smashed toys, curses, ridicule, and a complete lack of gratitude and respect are common.

The son or daughter, sitting in the midst of this and listening, literally doesn't bat an eye and displays a bland, neutral, expressionless face, a relaxed body, and a sense of boredom. Yet he or she is curiously patient while the parents bare their souls. His or her passive, polite decorum is impressive, given the parents' descriptions and their bereft, desperate wits' end. People ignorant of this kind of family situation would find it hard to reconcile this presentation in the office with the belligerent, rude, arrogant, and aggressive child the parents describe. But if you focus on the *process* as well as the *content* of that session, two things are immediately apparent: for one thing, Mom and Dad really, really care about this. The energy that spews forth their intense emotions is striking, especially when contrasted with their child's apathy. Also apparent is their child's lack of caring, minimal energy, and lack of emotion. But that child *is listening* to his or her parents—oh, not every word, but he or she is getting the gist *and hears loud and clear that they care.*

Because it does not provide the parents with any leverage, this session is counter-therapeutic; it also encourages the very behavior and attitude the parents are trying to extinguish in two ways. First, it focuses yet more attention on their child's inappropriate ways, lending further validity to the idea that he has the power to reduce his parents to sniveling idiots (i.e., the power to push their buttons). Second, it reassures their child that he is still loved. The energy and depth of their emotion, negative though it is, reinforces their caring—their love—for him. (This is the huge mistake that you make by yelling at and arguing with your child; these are displays of emotion that reveal how much you care, emotional engagements that reassure your child that he has an impact on you and that you love him no matter what. None of this has the power of simple neutrality, *the absence of emotion*.) And so the process of the session serves as reassurance that everything is, really, all right. No worries. As long as the child hears and sees how much the parents care about him—BINGO!

So why bother changing? What's truly in it to induce their child to change? At this point in a psychiatric evaluation of the context in which the child's defiant attitude and destructive behaviors are occurring, everyone is in agreement. Parents, child, and shrink all realize that the parents really have no leverage to bargain with. Their relationship with their child has moved beyond a problem—that their child is out of their control—and into the new power struggle to determine who will cave first. It is now a matter of principle and ego. The child realizes her parents have no true influence over her—and indeed they don't.

All the hints and techniques you've been taught fail because they *all* make the same mistake. They fall short. They will *not* address the elephant in the room, the unspoken, automatic, hard-wired connection—or the tacit agreement—between parents and their children that no matter what their child does, they will still love him unconditionally.

The essential mistake of the secrets and techniques you've already tried is this: they do not address the inappropriateness of *continued* unconditional love as your child advances in age. (Please read that sentence again. It is the most important one in this chapter.)

Erik Erikson, a developmental psychologist popular in the first half of the last century, is famous for his psychosocial stages of development, articulating the balance between trust and mistrust, autonomy and doubt, and rebellion and conformity as essential for normal development. (If there is any manual that should pop out of the womb along with the baby, it's Erikson's stages of psychosocial development.) We can use the first stage in Erikson's theory of growth and development to illustrate a precise analogy of the mistake embedded within these other techniques, the mistake that, after you think you've tried *everything*, is the reason you're reading this. This stage is referred to as Trust versus Mistrust.

Starting a few months after birth, the normal infant-parent relationship is tasked with establishing the bond between, usually, the mother and the child. The essential requirement for forming this bond is the mother's consistency. The more consistent she is in responding to her child's needs — that is, the more reliable she is — the stronger that bond becomes. Her unconditional reliability encourages her child's trust. If her baby had a stopwatch, the baby would find that mom responds to, say, his hunger cry after four to six minutes. Her consistently bringing the breast or bottle to him creates the expectation that he will have to wait about five minutes — if the baby has to wait at all — before crying or fussing produces the milk. For the next twenty months or so, the baby trusts that she might delay about five minutes before the next feeding. (Interestingly, the presence or absence of a delay is not the most important factor; it's the consistency that is crucial. If Mom chooses to not delay, then she'd best never delay. Giving her some slack, if there is a delay, it should happen in a consistent fashion, with a consistent amount of time involved.)

Now, recalling that this Eriksonian stage is called trust versus mistrust, a short lecture is in order. Each of his stages include "versus." This is not meant to label the word on the right as bad or the word on the left as good. As with the adolescent struggle with conformity versus rebellion, "versus" refers to the *balance of one and (versus) the other*. The healthy adolescent experiences both the need to conform to authority and the need to rebel or test the limits of rules, policies, and parental desires. If he becomes too rebellious or too conforming, the imbalanced youth runs a risk of sociopathy on the one hand and rigidity on the other, lacking a healthy separation and individuation from his or her family.

I had a sixteen-year-old patient who had a 4.0 GPA and graduated high school in three years, who was the football team captain and valedictorian and was voted "most likely to succeed," who was president of the student council, and who spontaneously helped with chores at home. There was not a blemish—a son you'd die for. Well, he killed himself with a .22 pistol pointed behind his neck at his brainstem. His suicide note included being exhausted from perfection, dreading the rest of his life living up to that standard, and wanting his parents to have a neat, open casket. No. You don't want an all-conforming adolescent on your hands.

In the trust versus mistrust stage, as the infant is nearing two, a mother might slip a bit, responding a beat late to the infant's hunger cry. (Her reliability might become less than unconditional, say, if she has a second child, just born.) Imagine the child checking her stopwatch: "Hmmm, five minutes late, should be here by now... hmmmm, what the hell? Here I am, starving. Where is she?" And as she continues to cry, she manages, accidentally at first, to touch her thumb to her lips, discovering the self-soothing act of thumbsucking. If she was capable of conscious self-reflection, she might think, "Well, this will have to do until she gets the milk over here. I can't leave this crib and find her, but I *can* suck my thumb." And this chips away a bit at the total trust she had, allowing not only some healthy mistrust of her mother in the future but also the discovery of some self-reliance—the ability to make do, with her thumb.

This is an example of the human condition known as frustration. Just as the seventy-five-year-old widow severely mourns her wonderful husband of fifty-seven years (a man who put her on a pedestal and took care of her every need and whim) and who now sorely misses his caretaking and must learn to face the world on her own, most of us have to deal with life's frustrations. As parents, we have the opportunity to gradually and safely introduce the concept of frustration into our child's awareness. But by unconditionally loving her, we don't take advantage of this opportunity. Instead, we expect her to accept our unconditional love—without ever being frustrated—until she's out in the real world and about to get a rude awakening.

This is the mistake present in the other well-meaning theories attempting to guide you in correctly parenting your child. They fail to point out that the parent is not there just to nourish the child; the parent is also there to ease the child into the often frustrating reality of our world.

Because the existing theories and techniques don't address the presence of and the inappropriateness of indefinitely loving your child unconditionally, they, in effect, insert a handy *escape clause* into any contract you make with your child. It's like the seventy-two-hour grace period that mortgage refinance contracts give you. If you change your mind, you can back out of the contract. The bottom line of any contract is a quid pro quo. You commit to some agreement involving other people. If you commit, you get a house or a car. With your child, both you and the child are agreeing to abide by the terms of the contract. Your side of the contract must involve finding a point of leverage with your child. With no leverage, why would your out-of-control child bother agreeing to the contract? When you say, "I've tried everything, and nothing has worked," what you're essentially saying is *you failed to find that point of leverage with your child.* (If you had, you wouldn't be reading this because the last book you read would've worked out for you and your child.)

Reading this, however, will tell you what the others don't. I can understand why the contracts they proffer all have escape clauses, and I understand why they don't bother to tell you that they do. They all have escape clauses because they're too scared *not* to have a built-in contract waiver; they don't tell you about the waiver—which is never directly mentioned—because, in addition to wanting to sell books, they do not want to admit that their technique and their strategies ultimately chicken out.

The built-in escape clause is this: no matter how awful things are between you and your child, he is still your child; you are still his mom, his dad. You've heard it and said it yourself: "Of course I love him. He's my son!" "I love him to death. I'm his father!" Therefore, if push came to shove, if worse became the worst, the simple fact of your biological, foster, or adoptive connection (all of which are tangible, discrete, and legal) will provide you with the clause allowing you to renege from your contract. Because of the ostensible connection, you will maintain warmth, emotional acknowledgment of him, and acceptance of him as emotionally worthy of you. No matter what he does, you will be emotionally responsive to him. That is the escape clause, the clause allowing you to maintain an active, ongoing emotional connection with him no matter what he does. The other strategies chicken out; they do not suggest that you remove yourself emotionally from your child and temporarily suspend all signs of emotional availability when you've completely had enough. *(Under no circumstances must your heart yield to your logic.)*

And guess what? It's not your child who uses this escape. It's *you*.

Sixteen-year-old Devon is in jail for the sixth time for an MIP (Minor In Possession of alcohol) and disorderly conduct. It's two o'clock in the morning. Do you bail him out? Of course you do. You're his dad!

Fourteen-year-old Kayla objects to your reminding her of the consequence of her failing to fill her part of your contract; she will not get to stay overnight with a friend because she failed to apologize for kicking her grandmother. In the car she yells, "Fuck you, you bitch!" while waiting for you to come to a stop at the red light. She suddenly opens her door and bolts—in the rain, without a coat. Even though it's only half a block from home, you notice she starts running in the opposite direction. Do you chase after her? Of course you do. You're her mom!

Seven-year-old Erin screams at your refusal to get her a cell phone. In Walmart, you've got a scene on your hands. People are staring. Erin is crying, sobbing, lying on the ground, and kicking her feet. You buy the phone. She shuts up, hugs you, and laughs with delight. All is well, right? You get into the car, and she insists on opening it. Despite your plan to give her what she wants now, but later, once at home, telling her she's not going to keep it, you notice how pleasant she is in the car now. Now that she has what she wants, she's all respect and joy. Shouldn't you reward this good behavior? Shouldn't you let her keep the phone? Of course you should. You're her mom!

The *quid pro quo* in these vignettes should be mutual cooperation. In each case, the child breaks a rule of the contract, thereby incurring the consequence, whether it be jail, not visiting a friend, or not keeping the phone. However, in each case, something popped up that suddenly brought the contract's existence—and validity—into doubt. Although the child failed to cooperate—and therefore failed to keep his or her part of the contract—the parent suddenly found an excuse to void the contract: a night in jail, running in the rain, delight about the phone—these circumstances can cause the parent to void and escape the binding of the contract.

But over and beyond these escape mechanisms you use is another much more powerful reason why you renege on your contract with your child. You renege because there is no strategy out there telling you that it's okay to resort to the one thing you've avoided: taking that tangible connection out of the picture. After all, what does an ovum or a sperm have to do with raising a child to be an adult who's tolerable to our society? Similarly, what does a title—adoptive mom or foster dad—have to do with helping a child understand the world? From an emotionally logical viewpoint, those connections mean everything loving and warm. But from the business-of-parenting viewpoint, they might actually get in the way.

In fact, the reason other strategies have failed is that they don't tell you to remove those factors from the contract with your child. Put another way, yes, *you are entitled to treat your child like any adult you'd have to deal with whom you can't trust.*

Your insistence on holding those ties near and dear to your heart allows you to avoid treating your child as you would treat anyone else you can't trust. This "specialness" is the tacit agreement between you and her to see the bond of biology or adoption as cause to never shut yourself off emotionally from your child. This special ingredient, which is the one-way street of unconditional love, is what thwarts your ever gaining the leverage you need to re-empower yourself and bring your child back into control. But this specialness exists not just because you care about her, but also because you care about yourself. You insist on this escape clause because you couldn't bear the guilt you know you'd feel

The Tyranny of Unconditional Love

were you to cut the bullshit and deal straight out with your child. So much anxiety is associated with the fear of this guilt that you are not willing to go that extra step to finally show your child what could *really* be at stake here: removing yourself emotionally from her life and being physically present but emotionally absent.

Put another way, you are loving your child too much, letting your heart override your sanity. You are caring too much, and therefore, you are at your child's mercy. The flow of love is so engulfing, so encompassing, that you—and your child—get distracted from the whole point of the parent-child relationship. Isn't the point of all this the maturation of your precious one into a responsible, mature adult? Yet you think that piling on the unconditional love no matter what your child does—at age four and seven and eleven and fourteen—will accomplish that?

Loving your child without condition will not encourage him to respect you. It *will* encourage further disrespect, because you're showing inadequate respect for yourself. The older your child gets with this stuff in the way, the harder it becomes to wrestle things around, and the more mutual bitterness, resentment, and disrespect there will be in your relationship.

> None of the techniques you've read or heard about take unconditional love *out* of the pic ture, suspending the unconditional, positive regard for your child.

None of them. No matter how tough your love, no matter what you think you've learned about not getting your buttons pressed, no matter how much you think you've stayed forty-three steps ahead of your child, you simply haven't read the small print in your contract: *"Under no circumstances shall you depart from the human being's need for acknowledgment and social interaction. No matter how bad your child treats you, your continued emotional presence to him or her is sacrosanct."*

Doesn't this put you between a rock and a hard place? You know not to let your daughter push your buttons, but you are worried that you won't react positively to her when she treats you with respect? You *do* want to reinforce her good behavior and respectful attitude, don't you?

The Crucial Moment

Your son screams at you for serving lima beans. He responds to your insistence to eat them by throwing them all over the place. You drag him to his room for a time-out, saying something like, "And don't you come out until you can treat me with more respect, young man!" Less than fifteen minutes later, he comes out, gently climbs onto your lap, and snuggles. You see a sad, sorry look on his face as he hugs you. Is that a tear he's wiping off his face? He says, "I'm sorry, Mommy." *Now this is more like it.* Wow. And here it is, the precise moment, the crucial point, and you don't even know it. You decide to be receptive to this hug. You tentatively hug back. (Stop reading for a moment. Imagine NOT returning his hug. Unthinkable, isn't it?) After all, he's no longer angry, demeaning, and dissatisfied with you, and he seems to regret what he did just a little while ago. Gee, he's certainly acting better now, his attitude more like it should be. You feel the tension seep away from him and from you, and the whole house feels nice again. Don't you reinforce this? He then asks you for the ice cream you'd promised for after dinner (after he ate the beans, which he didn't), his voice soft and frail. What will happen if you deny him the ice cream? Do you want another scene on your hands? After all, he *is* apologizing. Shouldn't this be rewarded, to accentuate the happiness? He's happy; you're happy. Sure enough, he gets the hug and the ice cream, and he gets happy. All is well. Now that he's happy, the whole house is happy.

Do you know what's wrong with this picture? Three things. First, your son sees the temporal connection here: he goes from angry to happy, and then *you* go from angry to happy. You screamed at him for not eating his lima beans. He screamed back

The Tyranny of Unconditional Love

at you, "You're mean, bitch!" But now he's not screaming, and you're not screaming. His anger triggered your anger; his happiness triggers your happiness. I'm telling you that he realizes, on some level, that he was the reason for your sadness and anger and that he is the reason why you then became happy. And he knows this because you give him this powerful information. You are connected enough to him and his feelings when he is irritable, defiant, rude, and angry, and then you show him that you are connected to him and his feelings now that he's happy. You reacted to both of his moods. In order for you to react, you must be invested in what he's doing. You care, and it shows.

Second, this vignette has little to do with the task and goal of parenting. Ironic, isn't it? It does, however, have a lot to do with the power struggle between the two of you. (In our field, we call it "the dance.") By reacting positively to his sudden mood reversal, you've essentially forfeited the power struggle *and* advertised a very poor short-term memory. He just had a good lesson in how to wrest control from you and was simultaneously not taught the value of good manners at the dining table (recall the lima beans). Essentially, you let him rob you of both the opportunity for you to parent him—to show him how others might react to his poor manners at mealtime—and to teach the practice of not wasting food, not to mention the healthy practice of eating his vegetables. I could go on and on. Even if you remind him of what he did some twenty minutes ago, it now doesn't matter. Because of your following his lead, now glad—whew!—that he's in a good mood, you have in fact showed him that his tantrum twenty minutes ago was **free**! It's all okay; after all, Mommy still loves him. And when he pushes it by then asking for that ice cream, Mommy confirms that all is well. The tantrum—and not eating the lima beans—wasn't a big deal after all. (You say, "But, Doctor, I've already tried this. I don't respond to his hug. I give him the cold shoulder. It. Does. Not. Matter to him." Then I reply, "Ah, so you understand this concept, but how long do you maintain that cold shoulder? Do you wait until he shows true remorse for his tantrum? Do you respond to that tantrum by giving him one in return, at a neutral moment, say, a week later? Do you let him know you won't respond to positive ploys for a good while and that the crucial moment *will linger*? I bet not." And I'd wonder how you define "cold shoulder.")

Getting back to that crucial moment, once you give him the ice cream, your moment has already passed. Is this the point those other books and strategies hold as the crucial moment? Without even considering your prediction of his reaction to your denying him the ice cream, which in itself might tell you how powerless you really are, please understand that the crucial moment has already passed. You've **already** informed him that, yes, Mommy still loves him and everything is all right, really.

The crucial moment was when he climbed onto your lap, approaching you with a hug. If the other books and strategies had focused on *that* moment, you wouldn't need to read this now, because you would've already known that that moment was your escape clause — not your son's or daughter's, but yours. You would have grasped that moment and opted not to reciprocate with a hug (opted *not* to escape the contract). But by reciprocating with a hug, you escaped from the contract, the purpose of which was to gain back some leverage.

But there's still a third thing wrong with this vignette. Topping all of it are the real reasons for his coming out of his room in a better mood. One reason was probably (you hope) subconscious on his part — he wanted reassurance from you that you still love him, that you still accept him, and specifically, that he did nothing that pushed you emotionally away from him. Meekly walking out of his room, wiping away a tear, and climbing onto your lap, approaching you with open arms and wanting hugs — this is that crucial moment. He was subconsciously — at age five or nine — seeking reassurance from you that you still love him.

The other reason he came out of his room without anger was conscious and deliberate: he wanted the ice cream. If the reason he had come out of his room with no anger and looked meek and sorrowful was that he regretted how he treated you while disputing the lima beans, you wouldn't be reading this book, because you would already have taught him the value of a sincere apology and the value of making amends. In order to feel sorry for calling you a bitch, he would've already learned empathy and the importance of putting himself in another's place.

Right now, you might be asking, "How old does a child have to be in order to be so crafty?" Maybe you can envision a sixteen-year-old enjoying her prediction that her mom has short-term memory problems, in effect forgetting all about the bad scene less than half an hour ago at the dinner table. Maybe a thirteen-year-old would feign remorse in order to still get the ice cream her tantrum a half hour ago should've prevented. But that's the wrong question. The correct question you should be asking is this: "How *young* does a child have to be in order to *not* be so crafty." If your thirteen- or sixteen-year-old is this crafty, don't you think she achieved a subconscious (or conscious) awareness of her skills years ago? The sequence of events starting at dinner and ending with your child enjoying the ice cream is a function of the dyad—you and your child subconsciously colluding to make sure this remains a part of your relationship. And it began way before you can imagine.

Both of you are invested in this dance: Let's forget what you did at the dinner table a half hour ago; I will reward your faked remorse for that behavior. You're still okay. (In this dance, you're colluding with your child to keep things going as they are and to protect him from your misgivings about him.)

That's just like the mom who reminds her child to settle down and sit still in our waiting room, only to forget to watch him a moment or so thereafter and who then has to remind him again and again to settle down. Is this the job security of remaining a nagging mother? The next time you're in a situation with children and parents that involves waiting for something, there's bound to be an overactive child scampering around and making noise, his mom busy talking with another adult. People are getting annoyed with her rambunctious child. She turns and says to him, "Quit it, Michael!" And he stops. She resumes her conversation and, sure enough, precious Michael goes right back to it. She again turns around: "Michael! Didn't I tell you to quit it?" (Does she ask him that because she forgot whether she did or not?) And he stops again. And on and on. What in God's name makes this happen? Should these people be shot?

Well, we can't shoot 'em, but we can understand them. Focus not on the content of the vignette, but its process, not what it is specifically about, but what the *doing* of it represents. This particular situation is a good example of why some people choose to become parents. You might know some of these people who need to become parents, whose identity is being a parent, and who are subconsciously afraid of having to *stop* being a parent. It's like the mom in this case wants to be stuck in time with her child, her mother role forever secure because, as everyone can see, her child needs to be constantly redirected. Obviously he can't mind his manners all on his own. He needs his mom.

And she needs him to forever need her to be his mom. She chooses this power struggle with him instead of raising him. It's like she's putting his growth and development on hold so that she can feel safe and secure that her role as mother will never end. Both mom and son are heavily emotionally invested in continuing this dance. And the irony is that it's not the son who instigates this; it's the mother. It would take a remarkably precocious and mature child to see what his mother is doing to him, as if asking her, "What did I do to deserve this? Must I continue acting regressed just to lower your anxiety, Mom? Is what we're doing really acceptable to the other people having to endure this? Mom, aren't you getting embarrassed here? I sure am!" This child might intuit that your agenda for failing to raise him is not because you unconditionally love him, but because not being a parent terrifies you.

And then when they're in my office, Mom essentially tells me, "Here. You do what I choose not to do. I refuse to give my child an accurate model of the real world. I can't control him; and, by the way, your waiting room is a mess."

A final note about that crucial moment: it is important that you treat that moment with respect and sincerity. Your "cold shoulder" must carry weight — heavy, quiet, clear, somber weight. Your facial expression reflects the sadness and hurt you feel at your son's behavior and attitude. Your eyes have a sad, preoccupied look because you are concerned. *How did things ever get this far?*

How much have I ignored your need to be raised right? I focused on the wrong things.

And your body language exudes a sense of *leave me alone now. I'm done.*

Believe me, if you're truly introspecting at this point, fearlessly examining your own agenda, you *will* look preoccupied and distant. As you should, because this is the situation you—and only you—can fix.

CHAPTER 5

WHY YOUR PARENTING STRATEGIES DON'T WORK

IF A PLUMBER comes to your house and fixes a broken water heater, and three days later you notice a decrease in water pressure in your basement sink, you might wonder, *Gosh what are the odds of two plumbing problems occurring in three days?* He used that very sink to test the temperature of the hot water coming from the water heater he just repaired.

To say he caused the second problem is paranoid. But to wonder if he spotted it during his first trip to your home, knew it would manifest itself soon, and didn't bring it to your attention so that he could charge you for another trip to your house — might not be paranoid. Using this as an analogy for these parenting books and techniques that fail, do they intentionally fall short so that you continue spending money on them?

Nope. I firmly do not believe that is possible. They're not intentionally withholding the secret that I'm suggesting to you here. And I say that because what I'm suggesting to you is simply too scary and too far out for them to embrace. In many cases—where a child is abused or severely neglected and didn't know ANY love, for example—a favorite reason for not going there is this: "Well, Josh has been through enough abuse and neglect. He doesn't know any love. Why should we subject him to more of the same abuse?" Is this good reasoning? Does this twelve-year-old whom you rescued from an abusive foster home that gave him no affection and only taught him to disrespect adults deserve *more* neglect?

No. He doesn't. But that's not the point. The adoptive parents who resort to this line of reasoning are focusing on what happened to Josh in the past and how it traumatized him. Well, okay, focus on that; it underlies Josh's depression, his reactive attachment disorder, and his anxiety. He definitely needs help with his awful past. But this has *nothing* to do with how he's treating his adoptive parents *now*. If anything, they feel sorry and perhaps guilty for what he went through. But the parents' job is not only to provide succor and nurturance; it's also to carefully raise the child and to provide an accurate picture of what it means to be an adult, what the world expects of us, and the quid pro quo nature of the human condition. One has nothing to do with the other. *Do not make the mistake of seeing lenience as a wise compensation for a child's traumatic past.* It isn't, no matter how bad the trauma was or how severe the emotional neglect. Plus, if he suspects your lenience, he will likely milk it for all it's worth. (If your child doesn't, you wouldn't be in the situation you're in now.) *He will think that his traumatic past is your Achilles heel.*

I've seen this happen in many families, not only with mentally ill children and teenagers, but also with the adult children of parents unwilling to let go. I've also seen it in families with developmentally disabled children of all ages. I gave you the example of Jared, the eleven-year-old child diagnosed as bipolar, whose mom blamed herself for passing the "bipolar gene" to him. I have more examples.

Tom is twenty-seven, manic psychotic bipolar, and still living at home. Though he did fine when he took his lithium, he often decided just to stop taking it. (A common reason for manic bipolar patients deciding to stop their meds is the natural high they feel when manic. They don't want lithium to kill the buzz.) Over the years, he had repeatedly stopped his lithium, which caused his mania to blossom, which caused him to do very impulsive and regressed things...things that invariably cost his parents money for damages he would cause and traffic violations he'd incur. Every time, his parents would plead with me to "do something for him." After the fifth instance, I recommended that they kick him out of the house if he relapses again because of lithium non-adherence. His father deferred to Mom, who began sobbing, explaining the guilt she felt for "raising a bipolar kid." It wasn't until the eighth episode—involving totaling the family car, getting into debt with two pimps, and a police car chase—that Mom and Dad kicked him out. Tom eventually adjusted to a halfway house and never stopped taking his lithium again.

Leah, a forty-five-year-old moderately mentally retarded female living in a sheltered environment run by a developmental disability agency, required daily assistance with personal needs and the activities of daily living. She did well and was very cooperative with the care she received from the caring staff. But when funding was cut and she had to share her apartment with another woman, Leah reacted to having to share her space by having temper fits when her druthers—say, to not have to wait until her roommate's food was completely done in the microwave—were thwarted. Leah especially minded having to forego her favorite TV shows, to the point where the staff begged a psychiatrist to place her on a mood stabilizer because of these "mood swings." After developing a life-threatening rash from Lamictal and damaging her liver with Depakote, she finally (barely) tolerated another mood stabilizer and seemed less reactive to frustration. But it wasn't until she completely destroyed the 3-D home theater system, which came with the new roommate, that the staff listened to reason. Leah was bipolar, *and* she was an only child who, after forty-five years, simply could *not* adjust to sharing with another person. Being mentally retarded certainly didn't help her frustration tolerance, but it didn't cause it either.

These examples show the real problem, the driving issue. It is not a chemical imbalance, nor is it mental retardation. Don't people with mental retardation or mental illness deserve to be raised correctly, too? Jared, Tom, and Leah made the choice to give other people a hard time. They chose not to cooperate with other people. Jared relied on his mother's intense guilt, Tom intuited (correctly) that periodically stopping his lithium would prolong his dependence on his parents, and Leah developed a bad case of sibling rivalry.

Tom's case was particularly difficult because his medication noncompliance caused a protracted adolescent delay in separating and individuating from his parents, and his protracted adolescence caused him to "rebel" by not complying with his medication treatment regimen. His parents were faced with a dilemma: how do you dare kick your son out of your house when he is so ill? And making this even more difficult was Tom's prolonged dependence on his parents. He seldom bathed, dressed, or fed himself. Period. How can you kick your son out when he can't even prepare his own meals? Here I am telling you to emotionally distance yourself from your adult child to the point where you are evicting him from the warmth of your home, when he is both mentally ill *and* functioning at barely more than the level of a six-year-old. You might be asking yourself, "How could I be so cold? I'd be freezing him out emotionally as well as physically. Could I possibly remain empathic to his mental illness, teach him daily living skills, *and* kick him out all at the same time?"

These examples illustrate several points. Both Tom's and Jared's moms felt guilty about somehow causing their sons to be bipolar, so they overcompensated for that guilt by avoiding the task of parenting their sons. They thought that by overcompensating, they were showing their sons more love. But they were really trying to feel less guilty about their belief that they had caused their sons' illness. When you act in such a way that you're trying to lower your guilt feelings, you are actually being quite selfish, taking care of your own anxiety. This has nothing to do with loving someone. So not only were they not appropriately taking care of their children, but they were actually taking care of themselves. The point is that parenting is a selfless—unselfish—activity, and quite often you, as a parent, don't receive the gratitude you deserve, because you're more often than not thwarting your child's wishes. Tom wanted to forever remain dependent on his parents. *That* was his reason, although completely subconscious, for skipping his meds. Relapsing, for Tom, meant prolonging adolescence and avoiding growing up. Once his parents thwarted that subconscious—perhaps somewhat conscious?—wish, after months of trying to get them to take him back, he managed to push beyond the recidivism, and he stayed on his meds and lived his life.

One very big reason, I believe, that existing strategies fail to address the inappropriateness of prolonging unconditional love is that doing so brings us uncomfortably close to examining our own ambivalence about our children. Ambivalence—having both positive and negative feelings for the same person at the same time—is a basic fact of the human condition. The task of parenting is so complex that we're bound not only to feel overwhelming joy toward our children, but also to feel overwhelming anger toward them. Although this is quite healthy, many parents can't bear the thought of being enraged at their kids, so placing the kids in a category of complete, unconditional positive regard can allow the parents to deny their anger toward them. *After all, she's my daughter. He's my son. Of course I love my children.*

Another reason why these strategies fall short on purpose, I believe, is that they're following the trend of the past half century of overprotecting and overindulging our children. We see it everywhere. My best friend and his wife recently celebrated their first child's first birthday party, and one of the gifts was a helmet. A nephew asked him, "What is that? Why did she get a helmet?" My friend responded, "Because she's gonna be walking soon." If you're old enough to remember (and if you're not, just ask your parents), back in the day, there were no helmets, kneepads, elbow pads, wrist protectors, seat belts, or car seats. How the hell did we survive?

This overprotectiveness is also illustrated in the reactions we now have to casual statements a child might make. If your child uses the word "bomb" in the context of a disagreement with another child, the school, the police, social services, and the judicial system are sure to get involved. If your child's doodling even hints at anything remotely aggressive or self-injurious, there's sure to be an investigation. Will your child begin to realize the power he or she has with mere words? Duh. (A very gifted ten-year-old ADD patient of mine thought it quite funny to leave a sticky on his school desk with the words, "I have balms in my locker. I dunno what to do." Another student spoke the words out loud, and both she and my patient were suspended for three days. My seeing the humor in it didn't go over well with the school, and quite seriously, I had to write a letter pronouncing both of them non-dangerous to anyone.)

To be clear, I understand the swing of the pendulum, from the days of child labor and the untold abuse. Yes, it's more than reasonable that the pendulum has swung far in the other direction. But we have become a society of wimps—frail, fragile folk with frail, fragile, and easily offended children, all of whom have to win, have to be special, and have to be *safe*, and who must be rewarded just for their very being.

And so the techniques and strategies you've already become familiar with are all heavily on the side of coddling your child, no matter how tough the love they suggest you try. To suggest suspending your unconditional love for your child may jolt some people, including the authors of the books you've read and the techniques you've tried, into a sense of rage and disgust at the mere idea of getting real with your child. Parents persist in denying the reality of our world in and through their relationships with their children. (This is already evident in the workplace. The current thirty-something population of white-collar working people tends to be more entitled than a generation ago. Many of them don't have the same work ethic, even in the face of our continued merit system and our bureaucracy, where you're valued for what you do, not for who you are. Their parents' overemphasis on unconditionally loving them as children is now translated into smug, conceited young adults appearing almost phobic of hard work.)

Do I show my child that I'm somehow above the bureaucratic merit system by not modeling it for him in the safety of my home? Is my motive for embracing unconditional love really just my need to deny the reality of the harshness of our world? Living vicariously with my child, using the magical thinking that we're all innately worthy and good just because of who we are — as if demanding "accept me just for being me" — must be limited, because it's not fair to my child to delude him so. Would you want your fourteen-year-old child to *still* believe in Santa Claus?

CHAPTER 6

MENTAL ILLNESS

In my practice, I see children of all ages, some with pure ADHD and pure bipolar disorder. (By "pure" I mean there's no comorbidity—the presence of another mental illness.) Providing medication management for these patients is usually straightforward and rewarding, combining the science and the art of psychopharmacology. But many children I see have combinations of diagnosable mental illness: ADHD, bipolar disorder, schizophrenia, separation anxiety disorder, post-traumatic stress disorder (PTSD), reactive attachment disorder (RAD), oppositional defiant disorder (ODD), conduct disorder (CD), and major depressive disorder (MDD). One particular type of depression is called dysthymia, which might've been diagnosed as neurotic depression in the past. Usually the child has had some type of emotional trauma that occurred one or more years ago and has developed a mask of bitter resentment toward immediate family and school personnel, which subconsciously hides the child's depression. A particularly common scenario is the child—anywhere from three to sixteen years of age—being disappointed in the past, often by parental neglect. The child acquires a stepparent, has intense ambivalence toward the neglectful (often biological) parent, and takes her anger out on the family she lives with, say, her other biological parent, the stepmom, and siblings.

"It's better to be mad than sad" refers to our tendency to replace depression with anger because anger is an easier emotion to endure than depression (usually mixed with hurt, betrayal, and emotional neglect). Developing ODD—where the child redirects her resentment of, say, her biological mom into brash anger toward her stepmom and anyone else present—is common in my practice. The underlying dysthymia, that is, the chronic, aching sadness, must be addressed along with the ODD.

Another example is a child with PTSD, having been somehow molested or brutalized in the past and then using aggressive conduct in an attempt to master his persistent fears. Developing conduct disorder (CD) is a way the child could act out his anger toward the molester, thereby being in control of others to compensate for feeling so out-of-control ever since the original trauma occurred.

Hence, it is important not only to treat the obvious manifestations of the *presenting* problems—in these cases ODD and CD—but also to treat the *underlying* affectual and anxiety disorders (i.e., the *core* of the problems).

In cases where ODD and CD coexist with bipolar disorder and attention deficit disorder (with **hyperactivity** [ADHD] or not), the task is not only to treat the obvious presenting problems but also the (as we currently understand them) genetic issues at hand. Usually, this comorbid situation demands a more aggressive approach to the bipolar disorder and the attention deficit disorder occurring with the ODD or CD. Whereas in the examples where the child's environment is largely responsible for the dysthymia or the PTSD, the CD and ODD usually demand the more aggressive approach (with psychotherapy gradually addressing the depression and anxiety disorders).

In both scenarios, the child essentially presents with attitudes and behaviors he cannot control—those resulting from PTSD, dysthymia, bipolar disorder, or ADHD—along with attitudes and behaviors he *can* control—those diagnosable as ODD or CD. The child's parent is truly overwhelmed, often very unsure of the cause of instances of unexpected—or even expected—anger, tantrums, withdrawal, defiance, self-cutting, substance use, suicidal statements, poor grades, and aggressive behaviors sometimes requiring law enforcement intervention.

I need to mention those cases where varying degrees of mental retardation might also be present, not to mention the current popular diagnosis, autism or autism spectrum disorder (Asperger's Syndrome).

If we look closely at the Jared vignette, we see a boy sparking a temper tantrum designed to spite the office staff asking him to clean up after himself and put the toys back in the box. His agenda is to cause misery and be defiant, powerful, and nasty. Giving him as much benefit of the doubt as possible, we could say his bipolarity causes low frustration tolerance and seeming insensitivity to others, this genetic disorder causing him to regress to the age of four when stressed by the request to stow the toys. It is common for a "dysphoric hypomanic" (a stage including both manic grandiosity and dark rage) to present this way, his bipolar disorder making him think that whatever he does, all will be well, and he will prevail. He can't stop to recognize the downside of his behavior because he literally can't see any.

On the other hand, we've got an admittedly guilt-ridden mom overcompensating with him because she thinks it's unfair that she passed the bipolar gene onto him. He's a spoiled brat! Under any circumstance, he would react to a demand by becoming spiteful and noncompliant. So what do you do? (I saw an ADD father and his eleven-year-old ADHD son a few years ago and assisted with differentiating between attention-deficit driven behaviors and pure spitefulness. Dad told me that his relationship with his son had improved so much that it could handle Dad's asking him, "Well, son, was that tantrum your ADD talking or the brat talking?" Not only handle it, but derive humor from it as well.)

I recently saw a twelve-year-old girl who was repeatedly sexually molested seven years ago. She is obviously depressed, anxious, and fearful, but she is also enraged at her mom for not knowing about it and preventing it. (Molested children typically are more angry toward the parent who should have known than toward the perpetrating parent.) Her father sought help because she was cutting on herself, torturing the cat, pulling her sister's hair out, making suicidal threats, and threatening her stepmother by telling her she'd "get her" in the middle of the night when commanded by voices to kill her. In this case, we have a seriously disturbed girl with severe PTSD and/or schizophrenia, who immediately needs medications in order to avoid lethality and hospitalization. On the other hand, we have a young girl holding the family hostage because of her unresolved anger toward her biological mother. She is the most powerful person in that family, and she wants someone to pay for her misery.

And then there's the seventeen-year-old jock wannabe whose grades plummeted to Ds and Fs, who couldn't focus or pay attention, who was constantly moving some part of his body, had extreme mood swings, smoked cocaine, had two DUIs, bullied the freshmen in school, stole from his parents, punched his mother, and laughed at his stepfather who was trying to be a better dad than the biological father. In this case, we have a young man who takes his anger toward his biological dad out on the rest of the family and advertises his depression and internal misery by inflicting pain on others. He is either ADHD or bipolar or both, but he refuses to take medications. On the other hand, we have a conduct disordered child who needs more stern parenting than his stepdad can provide.

My practice also includes nursing home patients as well as the developmentally disabled population. Elderly people with or without dementia are perfectly capable of displaying arrogant attitudes and aggressive behaviors. And no matter what the chronological age, a person with mental retardation can exhibit these behaviors, too. A combination of these issues with other illnesses, such as bipolar disorder, PTSD, and dysthymia, can produce very challenging cases indeed.

These cases illustrate the vexing challenge of trying to figure out which attitudes and behaviors are due to environmental neglect, which are due to a genetic defect, and which are due to pure spoiled entitlement based on a lack of respect for the parents (or other authority figures). And part of this challenge is, of course, that the *same* attitudes and behaviors can be caused by *all* of these factors. (A thorough and helpful discussion about specific combinations of mental illnesses and parental deficit is beyond the scope of this book, but I plan to address these issues in a second book.)

However, there are some common threads that run through most, if not all, of the possible combinations. As briefly alluded to early on, an essential difference between ADHD and a mood disorder such as bipolar disorder is the agenda that the problem behavior or attitude is addressing. In pure ADD or ADHD, the attention deficit really does interfere with the child's ability to comply with chores. One parent I see put it very well, saying, "He always looks like he *wants* to take the garbage out. There's no defiance, no lip." The child truly cannot carry the notion of doing the chore through from the moment it's requested of him, unwittingly getting distracted by everything in his environment. So the absence of the agenda to oppose his father is a clue that his not doing the chore is *not* due to any opposition-defiant agenda. In addition, the pure ADD child will most often sincerely apologize for disappointing his parent by not doing the requested chore. With varying mixes of ADD and, say, bipolar disorder, the absence or presence of an attitude designed to inform the requesting parent of *intentional resistance* is often the "tell" you can use to determine if your child has an audacious agenda behind his not doing the chore. The observed and sensed willingness to comply (or lack thereof) is often the best clue.

Another common thread is, of course, if your child happens to defy or abuse *only* you when her wishes are thwarted. Although it might be tempting to think that this is always due to ODD or CD—rather than, say, ADD or bipolar disorder—keep in mind that the child with ADD or bipolar disorder tends to garner certain responses from her environment that a child without those illnesses might not. For example, an ADD child might've let other kids down so often that they've come to exclude her from their social circles or perhaps not respond to her desires. This child would then risk developing oppositional defiant disorder *because of* her ADD — in order to compensate for the lack of control and potency she feels in social situations. I've seen many instances of an undermedicated ADHD child looking as if she has ODD, but when her Ritalin dose is increased, she begins to cooperate more with others, thereby improving other children's responses to her. The assumed ODD then vanishes — a good sign that it's an improper diagnosis. If, as postulated above, the ODD problems are directed primarily to *you*, this might alert you to your child's needing to make an increased conscious effort to behave appropriately around others, relaxing that effort when with you because she expects more understanding from you. This is a dicey situation, because it's one thing to kick back in the security of one's home, but if it takes that much conscious effort for her to compose herself, maybe her ADHD is under-medicated.

Other threads running through the various illness comorbidities include the timing of the attitudes and behaviors, the environments in which they occur, and the people with whom they occur. Of course, the presence of spite and revenge — having a derogatory point to make — tends to place a given attitude or behavior in the category of willful, self-directed, controlled, and targeted at specific people in specific circumstances. These variables can provide valuable clues as to the child's agenda, but a thorough discussion is beyond the scope of this book.

Finally, the presence of varying degrees of mental retardation is particularly challenging. Basically, the presence or absence of "secondary gain" can provide valuable clues. I often gently remind clinical staff (who are blessed with seemingly infinite patience and tolerance) who are working with the developmentally disabled population that an IQ has to be much lower than they'd think in order to render a person incapable of recognizing that he or she can manipulate them. This can be particularly difficult for parents and caregivers to grasp.

> The hardest part of the challenge
> is to know
> when and how to empathize with the
> illness-producing problems and when
> and how *not* to empathize
> with (i.e., enable) the relationship-
> producing problems.
>
> Showing your child love in spite of his or
> her mental illness is one thing.
> Mixing "of course I love you" into the
> midst of interpersonal strife is another.

Suicidal thoughts and "I wish I were dead!"

Daring to suspend our love in order to properly parent a child compels us to look at the issue of suicidality. In the midst of trying to distinguish between your child's mental illness—and the emotional pain it produces—and his willful oppositional defiance, many of you have likely dealt with this disturbing issue as well. Suicidality—the current term used to describe thoughts, feelings, fantasies, gestures, and attempts to either kill oneself or purposely harm oneself—can make your task of dealing with an oppositional-defiant child much more difficult. Many of you are undoubtedly experiencing these issues, which lately seem to be escalating in frequency among children and adolescents. (Making this even more of a challenge is the relationship between suicidality and antidepressants. Suicidality might in fact increase after beginning treatment for depression, anxiety, and mood swings.) This topic of self-injurious and suicidal behaviors has been extensively written about, so I need to address it in the context of this book's focus. Often there is a very difficult balancing act, on the one hand adopting a healthy emotional distance from manipulative behaviors and attitudes and, on the other, having sensitivity and compassion for the very real emotional and mental anguish that can lead a child or adolescent to such thoughts, feelings, and behaviors.

In the context of our topic and the parenting tools discussed, suicidal threats can be daunting. Tackling this issue head on, it's important first to step back and assess where you stand with your child. What's the status of your relationship? (A good question we don't ask each other often enough is "How are *we* doing?") Is your relationship contentious enough that your child would feel the need to trump you during an argument? (This assumes that you are still allowing your child to trap you into the hair-pulling, futile one-upmanship of arguing about anything and everything. In fact, if suicidality came up in the *absence* of chronic arguing, it might be more ominous—because your communication with your child has not been loud; rather, it's been stifled.) Whether your child makes a suicidal statement, threat, gesture, or attempt, the communication between you two has moved so much into the win-lose arena that self-injury seems like the logical next step. How else can your son get your attention?

This refers to your attention as a parent—not as a competitor, not as a one-upsman, and certainly not as the person with the last word (or last laugh). You don't put an emotional ten-foot pole between you and him to ignore him. In fact, by doing so you are giving *him* attention. You're not paying attention to *your* thoughts, feelings, quips, curses, or smartass comments. You are out of the picture as someone invested in winning an argument.

When suicidal or self-harm issues arise, you do in fact stop. (One thing you can count on is that the more verbal your child is with such sentiments, the less likely he or she is to *act* on these sentiments, because verbally expending the energy of the emotion tends to dissipate the urge to express it through violence.) He's got your attention, and you pay attention—*to the condition to which your relationship has deteriorated*. If you haven't already engaged his arguing, that's good. Tensions haven't maxed yet. You drop whatever the about-to-be-argued issue is and you collect the both of you, cognitively, emotionally, even in a hug perhaps, if it's not awkward at that moment. And you say—after reading through this example and <u>extracting what your particular style sees fitting for you, your child, and the moment</u>—the following:

The Tyranny of Unconditional Love

*"Whoa, Charlie! We're not doing good here, if you feel the need to resort to **this** to feel acknowledged. Let's both have a time-out right now. We mean much more to each other than attending or not attending a prom. If the only way we can get through this awful idea — your being so miserable that you've thought of THIS — is to let you go to the prom, then you should go. I am able to forego this opportunity to teach you a valuable thing about yourself and the world you're getting ready for. But I maintain that the behavior and attitude that got you grounded in the first place is still important and must be respected. If you do go to the prom, I still maintain that you did not earn it. And I owe it to you to prepare you: earning things in this world is the only way you get to have them and still be able to sleep at night. Next time, I want you to have the pride of earning what you want for yourself. THAT PRIDE is what you deserve, prom or no prom."*

This strategy allows you to maintain your dispassionate observation of the choices your child makes, but at the same time sets suicidality and self-harm issues apart from maintaining an emotionally aloof posture. They must be set apart, because this is a lose-lose proposition; if you pay attention to this issue, you run the risk of reinforcing the likelihood that it will happen again. If you ignore it, and your child acts out the sentiment, then you'll feel so guilty that you further disempower yourself down the road. Either way, you'd be showing your child that he really does have the power after all.

Get the prom out of the way. Remove the trigger that gave rise to the whole issue of suicide and self-harm. There's plenty of time after the prom. Reduce the prom's importance.

Two weeks after prom, in a neutral moment, you — and his father or stepdad — sit down with him, and you tackle the damn thing. You preface it with the fact that, yes, the suicidal content did grab your attention, you respect him for sharing his thoughts with you, and you need to spend some time together improving the parent-child relationship so that nothing is so disastrous that it has to get to that point again. Be clear on the central theme: earning or not earning privileges in the future. Your child does have the power and control to have what he wants, if he earns it. It is your duty to guide him to learn this valuable fact of life. Conflicts will continue to surface, but we need to do better. Together.

Distancing yourself emotionally from your child's internal stage-of-life conflicts might be, at least at first, used by your child as an awful assumption that you really don't care. If your child were to say, "I wish I were dead!" or "I wish I'd never been born!" these words semantically do not constitute actual suicidal thoughts, threats, or intent (to deliberately take one's own life). They *are* passive death thoughts or wishes, though, and should be appreciated and respected as representing your child's sudden desire to be anywhere else but right there in front of you. Thoughts and feelings of desperation and anger—usually on top of sadness, insecurity, and anxiety—can be verbalized in this manner. The **context** and **setting** in which they are uttered are, very often, the key factors leading you either to fear that these passive death wishes might become actual suicidal thoughts and plans OR to see them as hyperbolized, dramatic statements that your child can find no way around the dilemma. Listen to the actual words spoken, but also take the time to explore the troubling issue at the root of these words. (Children and adolescents have a knack for futurizing current dilemmas into "forever-and-ever dilemmas," seeing no way out. Ever. Understanding this might help you ease the angst they feel at that moment.)

But what if your gut tells you that your child's mental illness is not in play here—and the setting and context is your child simply not getting her way? What then? Perhaps her words are, at least in part, exaggerating her feelings of frustration and annoyance, she herself feeling disempowered at that moment. This makes sense, because her words—especially in today's supercautious atmosphere—are designed to make you stop. She's got your attention. Does she really find death more attractive than not having a new iPod? Is death the *only* way out of cleaning her room? Does she have a point here—that the context and the setting are a statement of *your relationship with her* forcing one of you to win and one to lose? The reason this is such a heated topic, aside from the potential emotional and physical casualties, is that it represents not only your child's choice of a tool to deal with her anger and loss of control, but it also represents the condition of her relationship with her parents.

> The best way to approach this issue is with anticipation and preparedness. Rather than putting out an alarming bonfire, examine a potential situation during a neutral moment, perhaps during a conversation with your child.

Nowadays, schools will react to just about any word or statement that even remotely hints at the possibility of danger to self or others, and this has both positive and negative implications. We can make use of this reality as a segue to a calm discussion with our children about this issue—dangerousness to self or others. Perhaps if another student has said or done something harmful to himself or another person, during a calm, neutral moment you might invite your child to mention any thoughts or feelings the event sparked in him. And I would encourage you to bring up the notion of true suicidal intent versus the need to "cry out for help" versus the need to make an impact on others. Invite your child to share his perception of the meaning of the event, maybe extrapolating to any guesses he has about what might be going on in that child's relationship with *his* parents...issues that compelled *him* to think of, speak of, or actually do harm to himself or others.

Such a discussion might shed some light on your child's relationship with you and her feelings about sharing thoughts and feelings about a sensitive topic. It might also illuminate where your child stands on this issue as far as her own views on cutting herself, ending her life, or even on just dying and being gone. What might compel *her*? Does she feel comfortable enough in this discussion with you to bring up a hot topic that might've already surfaced—right here and now in this neutral moment? (Whether she does or doesn't feel at ease doing this can tell you a *lot* about where you stand with her.) Can she think of deterrents to doing harm? A starting point might be imagining with her a possible area of contention, say, how she'd react if she did something that wound up grounding her, thus preventing her from attending prom. In essence, what is worth dying for? What is worth killing herself over? What is worth cutting on herself?

Self-mutilation—usually cutting, but sometimes burning with flame or abrasives—has symbolisms all its own. Very often, it is a controlled way of releasing anger, emotional pain, frustration, and feeling out of control over a conflict. Usually it is not suicidal in nature. Some cutting is purely on the basis of a mental illness; at other times, it's purely on the basis of spiteful vengeance. But most often, it's a combination of both. Regardless, self-cutting is a way to compensate for being out of control. (When a person cuts, he or she can control the amount of damage, see the product—skin damage and perhaps blood—and put a limit on the amount of damage done.) And a neutral moment would be a good time to encourage your child to let you know when the thought of self-harm might cross her mind. Not being able to go to the prom makes a teenager feel very out of control. Your dispassionate stance (the emotional ten-foot pole) to her tantrum must be *matched* by your attention to the core issue: control. We humans despair when we feel out of control. Whatever your child did for you to ground her in the first place can't be undone. She can't control that. So she instinctively grasps at anything she might be able to control, such as arguing with you about her current personal dilemma. She can't go back and undo what she did, but she might be able to control *you* now. If arguing with you might erase the grounding, of course she'll try it. But it has nothing to do with the original issue—her entitled agenda, for example, not to cooperate with a chore—which started the whole thing.

> Do you see? Following her lead
> into an argument is reinforcing her
> suspicion that
> she can recapture the control she lost
> when she made the wrong choice,
> which got her grounded in the first place.

Her mistake here is assuming that controlling you in an argument will erase the anxiety she feels *because she knows she caused herself to lose control over the prom in the first place.* So in this type of situation, your job is both to guide her through the angst of not going to the prom *and* to show her that arguing with you will *not* bring the prom back. Her suicidal or self-harm threats might force you into letting her go to the prom, but you didn't argue about it with her. You kept your dispassionate ten-foot pole functioning through all of this.

> It is important to soothe yourself
> in this situation.
> You must believe that letting
> her go to the prom
> is *not* your losing anything
> or being lenient.
> It is simply taking yourself
> as a deal-broker
> out of the picture. The bottom line is this:
> <u>She didn't earn the prom.</u>

I hope you see how this strategy takes you to a much different place with your child. Instead of wrangling about anything and everything, you stay focused on the parenting plan. Your relationship with your child will thus be strengthened enough to tackle life's real issues. How do any of us maintain any sense of control in our daily lives, *and* how do we handle ourselves when we're not in the control we want to be in? If you allow her to control *you* with arguing about anything and everything, you might make her think that *that* is the way she should always handle feeling out of control: to try to control others. This is teaching her to be externally focused and not internally focused. Instead, your obligation to her is to open her eyes to the fact that *she* has the power to regain her sense of control…without "winning" a thing over you or anyone else. (We refer to this as an *internal* locus of control.)

After all, wouldn't it be a helluva lot better for her to approach you with her insecurities about control issues than to meaninglessly try to control *you*? If she did, you could embrace the opportunity to share some of your own insecurities.

Crucial to this is focusing on your relationship with her. If she had to resort to a suicidal action, gesture, comment, or threat—or if she had to resort to self-harm in any way—this is a statement about where you stand with each other.

Your goal is *not* to make her feel out of control. My goodness, a child has enough reminders of that on a daily basis. Not going to the prom feels brutal to her *because* it makes her feel this way. Your task is not to rub it in her face but rather to help her mature. For her to focus on trying to turn the tables on you and make *you* feel out of control—with her suicidal or self-cutting issue—makes a statement about your relationship: that it has grown contentious and highly competitive. Rather than fight *against* each other, *why not fight alongside each other?* Both of you together tackling the demands and sometimes ridiculous rules that society puts on both of you? As if to say to her, "Megan, we're in this thing together. You and me."

See, it is precisely at this moment when you might share some power struggle you had at her age. Let's say she originally got grounded for not completing a science project for school. She understood the agreement, that she would risk getting grounded if she neglected this project. That would've been enough, of course, but the timing placed it right at prom time! I've seen so many parents use the "bad timing" excuse as an **escape clause**. "But it's prom time. We can't let her miss prom night! She'll never be sixteen again. Don't you see, Doctor?" (Thinking: *I love my child too much to make her miss the prom.*)

Of course, she didn't look ahead enough to realize that now is not the time to slack off in her school work. She's only sixteen, right? (If she did look ahead, thinking that prom would be her escape from getting grounded for not doing the school project, perhaps she's on to your using Christmas and birthdays as escape clauses.) But I ask you, what age *is* the right age for your daughter to experience the results of lack of foresight? Seventeen? Won't there be a prom in senior year? What then? At what age did *you* learn this valuable lesson? (It's funny, most of the lessons we learn are the results of our mistakes, not our successes.) Whether she goes to the prom or not, this is a golden moment to seize the opportunity to share your own experience with her.

> Sharing your own hard-learned lessons shows your humanness. Can you imagine crying, complaining, and even laughing at the same things? That's the kind of company that misery loves!

Of course, sharing your feelings with your child can extend to how you'd feel about her suicidality. Your dispassionate, emotionally-void **observing-participation** when your child is being oppositional and defiant is done very seriously, with no sarcasm, cynicism, or ridicule. You are not there to show him anger or spite. You are there to show him true sadness, hurt, and disappointment. You feel this way not only because of your child's attitude and behavior, but also because your relationship with him is disturbing. And it takes two to make it this way. So approaching your child's suicidality as a warning statement about where you stand with each other enables you to take responsibility for your half of the problem. Your child isn't threatening suicide right now just because it suddenly occurred to him as a way to trump you. The contentious nature of your relationship with him has been eating at him as well as at you. Yes, it would be nice if you're reading this before suicidality ever came up—and I hope most of you are — and if you are now confronted with it, now is a great time for both of you to heed the warning.

In the context of the tools I'm advocating here, might your child react to your emotional ten-foot pole by trumping it with suicidal or self-injurious statements, threats, drawings, or actions? This would be additional evidence of a contentious and competitive relationship steering your child in that direction. Again, I tell you to stop. Even though you've been paying even more attention to your child by not letting your own ego interfere with his development, at this moment you make it very plain that you respect his last-straw effort that warns both of you it's time to turn the relationship around.

If you've been asking yourself how it's possible to emotionally freeze your child out and still show willingness to love conditionally, handling suicidality in this way is a good example. It highlights your paying attention to your child's maturation while refusing to be held hostage by manipulative ploys.

By opening up a dialogue about the meaning of suicidality issues within your relationship during a neutral moment, you are showing your child that you are not in this for any conquest. You're not interested in winning at his expense. Rather, you're extremely interested in helping him learn how to deal with frustration, annoyance, anger, and control issues out there in the world. (And by choosing a neutral moment to bring up sensitive issues, you are going out of your way — instead of being forced into it by a looming bonfire — to pay serious attention and respect to your child and his viewpoint on such issues.)

But what do you say or do if a bonfire *does* occur? You and he are now at odds because you are standing by the consequence of a forfeited prom due to your child's prior behavior. He didn't earn the prom. You've adopted the technique of standing back and dispassionately observing the decisions he's made, and you've decided he will not go to the prom. He tries to argue the point with you. If you've taken my suggestions to heart, you will *not* engage in arguing with him. This all by itself might lower the risk of the *confrontation, which usually is the reason why a heated discussion can suddenly move forward to the suicidal/self-harm arena.* My point here is that this bonfire doesn't happen in a split second.

Replying to the points he's making by turning this into an argument between you and him will only make him feel more self-righteous and outraged because you are then confirming that it *is* a war between you and him.

And if he does advance to playing the suicidality card, you can assure yourself that he sees it as within the scope of your relationship with him. The countless prior arguments have convinced him — can you blame him? — that you're his adversary.

Remember, you are not there for yourself, to win anything or to prove your net worth to your child. You are there for *him*. And this can be very exhausting and painful, but you're in it for keeps. You love him — but that has nothing to do with the prom. Using unconditional love as *your* trump card at that point is *not* in anyone's better interest. If you do so, you would be teaching your child that suicidality will cause others to want to prove they love him unconditionally as a way to stop him from hurting himself.

Using your emotional ten-foot pole shows your child that you are not emotionally invested in having a fight with him to see who wins. You are there to help him navigate through the morass of feelings he has in the moment.

> Yes, you can avoid loving your child unconditionally *and* care for your child at the same time.
> True caring is stepping out of the conflict and mirroring the world for him.

It is precisely your stepping back and not arguing with your child that is the kind of love you want to show him and have for him. You are putting him first. You are not trying to egotistically trounce him. You are loving *him*, not yourself. And if you think about it, isn't *this* what unconditional love truly is? It's loving someone with no expectations that your love will be reciprocated.

Looked at from this perspective, stepping back and not arguing with your child isn't forfeiting anything. It's not giving up an opportunity to set him straight; rather, it's giving up an opportunity to draw attention to yourself.

CHAPTER 7

ELIMINATING THE ESCAPE CLAUSE

NOW BACK TO that interview of the mom and her child. After negotiating the complex issues of chemical imbalance versus willful misbehavior, here comes the most difficult, crucial point. I quietly explain to Mom that the role of parent is, actually, quite simple and straightforward. Your role as parent, I advise her, is to teach your child what our world finds tolerable and acceptable. You're already providing shelter, clothing, food, and emotional nurturance. The missing ingredient, which by its absence is the cause of all the difficulties, is to offer a model of the world and its expectations. You are the safest first presenter of a critical piece of reality that your child will be expected to know, namely, that being loved for who he is might be in his romantic future, but otherwise, he will be loved and accepted for what he *does* and how he treats others. *Your child depends on you to do this for him.* The key to helping your child improve is not to do anything *more* than you are already doing, or to try recommended strategies any *harder* than you already are. In fact, you must do much, much less.

Do much less than the arguments and power struggles with your child that engage him in making it a thing between you and him: who's right, who's wrong, your ego versus his ego, what he thinks of you, the labels he assigns to you, micromanaging his day, caught up in the content of his decisions—drugs or no drugs, truancy or not, curfew or not, chores or not, do as you say or not. These are conflicts between you and your child. They are not strategies for accurate parenting, which should offer a correct model of our world that your child can internalize. If all you're seeing is your child's attitude, behavior, and agenda as things to argue or debate, you're missing the point. And if your child knows that an escape clause is inevitable, she will relentlessly argue until it rears its lovable head. See, that's a major reason why you continue arguing so much: your child knows your weak spot, whether it's Christmas, or a birthday, or prom night… and she knows that if she persists long and hard enough, she'll manipulate you into acquiescing. *The mere fact of your willingness to argue displays your inability to resist the temptation to give in to an escape clause.* Therefore, the sooner you show her that there ARE no escape clauses, the quicker you'll avoid many of your future arguments.

I recently saw Karen, a thirty-eight-year-old depressed mother of a seventeen-year-old young man. She was upset because he was failing three subjects in junior year, which would cause him to disqualify for the prom and prevent his graduating a semester early next year. Part of her depression was due to his rarely speaking to her, his vaguely disgruntled facial expression, and his awkward kind of quiet. He recently ran away from home after an argument, which *she* started, about his poor school performance, she told me. But after listening a bit, it became obvious that she was more upset about his missing the prom and not graduating high school early. She recalled that her pregnancy with his older sister forced her to quit school in her junior year, thereby missing her own prom and graduation.

This example illustrates Karen's agenda to live vicariously through her son. It is *she* who can't bear the thought of his missing out on the prom. It is *she* who wants to make sure of graduating.

Now there's nothing wrong with living vicariously through our children. It's part of the joy of parenthood and childhood. And at first—from birth to about age two—unconditional love is a necessary part of it. But it's a tricky path to follow, and it must be well-defined and limited. Unconditional love must be limited and appropriate to the child's age. But love for your child is forever. It begins as unconditional and evolves into a mutual certainty that you love him, no matter how difficult life might be, no matter how many chores he does, no matter how much work it takes to teach him the rigors of our world. Your love must never be called into question—as if letting him have an unearned prom is necessary for him to know you love him. And with Karen here, inserting her agenda into her concerns about her son's graduating a year early gives him a handy escape clause: why should he do what *she* wants, anyway? (And he does have a point.)

The goal of successful parenting (like the goal of successful psychotherapy) is its own termination. When is our job of parenting done? When we dispassionately see that our child is self-accountable and responsible to operate in society with self-directed free will coupled with moral restraint. Dyads are complex relationships, as you know, and if we as parents stall our child's social and emotional development, our child will make sure we pay for it. As teaching college taught me, students are extremely sensitive to whether the teacher is up there for them or for his own agenda. The teacher who languishes in self-aggrandizement and who makes a point of trying to impress his students by amplifying the differences between him and them—"look how smart I am, how stupid you are"—will pay for this with the disrespect and ridicule his students retaliate with. The same is true with parents who make it clear to their children, whether overtly or tacitly, that they became parents for their own agendas rather than for their children's agenda. Karen's agenda is to attend classes, go to prom, and finish high school. Right now, it is not her son's agenda. Karen's good intentions—to encourage her son's success in school—are drowned out by her subconsciously trying to impose her agenda onto him.

Most of you know that the normal adolescent will struggle with mixed feelings about independence versus dependence on her parents—a facade of tough know-it-all covering a core of reasonable anxiety about eventual autonomy. Similarly, the younger child we are trying to raise has mixed feelings about it. On the one hand, she wants her parents to be lenient and forgiving; on the other hand, she yearns for the correct teaching of maturational skills.

Face it, your child will disrespect you if you do not empower yourself. You are now aware of that disrespect shown as his oppositional, defiant, and rude attitude and his uncooperative behavior. What you're not aware of is the disrespect your child feels, largely subconsciously, toward you because you're not doing your job. After all, is he supposed to raise himself?

And now I will tell you what the other theories won't, how the other strategies fall short. Embracing this requires you to fully understand that this is for your child's benefit, not yours. Under no circumstances should you approach this strategy with sarcasm or cynicism toward your child. What I'm about to tell you is the technique that finally takes YOU out of the picture. This is *not* a power struggle between you and your child. Rather, this is you observing the choices your child makes and then reacting as you would, for example, to a coworker.

How would you deal with a coworker whom you can't trust? Think about it. If you're reading this, aren't you in the awkward, apprehensive position of a parent who cannot trust his or her child? Are you reluctant to let your child know this? Could you tell your child, "Hey, Darren, we don't trust you. Y'got us dancin' around, walkin' on eggshells here. It's just not nice being around you, y'know?"

You might readily respond to how you'd deal with a manipulative, caustic coworker. You would display good awareness of the famous saying "Fool me once, shame on you. Fool me twice, shame on me." You would give that individual a wide berth, treating the person politely, in a businesslike way, cooperating with joint work tasks, but most importantly, erecting a dispassionate, emotional ten-foot pole.

Imagine that. Imagine observing your coworker in a dispassionate manner, devoid of or unaffected by passion, emotion, or bias. If you captured your face in a mirror, you'd see a calm, resigned expression registering a quiet resolve that you cannot allow yourself to trust him. Your facial expression suggests more of a looking inward than being mesmerized with his crafty skill. Many times, now, he has betrayed you, let you down after building you up, and disappointed you as firmly as if he knew your biggest Achilles heel. The disappointment shows in your facial expression, your eyes reflecting disbelief. "How could he?" you ask yourself, and then *"How could I?"* You see the sadness in your eyes, the downturn of your lips, the deflation and hurt.

And the anger...the annoyance, frustration, bitterness, and rage. You know it's there, and in your reflection, you see the depression underlying it. The person you wanted to trust, after repeatedly giving him the benefit of the doubt, let you down yet again. It is precisely that—the true bottom line of your sadness and hurt—reflected back to you in the mirror.

And it is precisely that with which you fashion your emotional distance, your emotional ten-foot pole. Not your anger, your need for vengeance, your need to retaliate in kind, or your willingness to argue about the details of a contract you made with him (the end result being a tacitly prearranged escape clause such as those you have with your kids). No. The sadness you see in your face— that is the real deal. You're done. You realize, "What's the point in trying anymore?" You've reacted in the past, showing your rage and retaliating, trying to make your coworker feel the way you feel, debating and arguing with him. Then he says he's sorry and treats you better for a while, only to set you up again as if you're a fool. Is there any point in repeating your past reactions to his lack of respect for you?

No, there isn't. And you are certain of that. You sigh with **acceptance** of the reality he's consistently shown you. You conclude that he's not someone you can trust, and you accept this as fact. No what-ifs, no bargaining; there's nothing you can do.

Elisabeth Kübler-Ross delineates five stages of grief—denial, anger, bargaining, depression, and acceptance—that constitute the "work" of bereavement. They don't necessarily occur in any order, and more than one can be felt at any given time. They are components of our emotional reaction to a loss of some kind—in this case, *the loss of another person's respect*. Oh, we try to get it back right away; we really want respect from that person. We argue our point, pleading to an invisible panel of infallible judges staring down at us, hoping that if we are earnest enough we will be granted respect by that other person and approval from imagined others.

But no matter how hard we try, we fail. Here I am telling you that there really is nothing further to try, nothing more you can do. And so, you do nothing. Nothing. Oh sure, you still have to be with him; he's still part of your environment, and you must deal with him. But other than that—that is, continuing the workday while treating him politely and with businesslike decorum—there's nothing else you do.

Outwardly, toward him, you're polite and neutral, mixing business with business. Inwardly, however, you are doing something. You're observing the choices he makes in his work relationship with you. Is he cooperative or not? Is he helpful or not? Does he show appreciation for your work or not? Does he treat you with respect or not?

These are things you observe. Emotionally you do *not* react to anything. You must be polite, thanking him when he does cooperate and quietly accepting when he does not cooperate. You sigh with acceptance of the reality that you cannot allow yourself to be emotionally present to him. You've concluded that he will again disappoint you, so you anticipate and expect nothing else, nothing more. Emotionally reacting to his again letting you down is *not* going to do anything but perhaps obtain a meaningless apology from him.

And—the most important part of your mental set here—your emotionally reacting to his suddenly helping you or cooperating with you or surprising you with an act of kindness is ALSO not going to change *his agenda* toward you. Do not make the mistake of assuming that showing heartfelt appreciation for any uncharacteristic kindness from him is what you can do to reinforce and reward such kindness. Think about this. He disappoints you, lets you down → you (emotionally) react with anger → he apologizes and does something kind for you → you (emotionally) react with glee → now, what do you think you've just reinforced here? The irony is that you have *not* reinforced his kindness—you haven't increased the chances that (*maybe now?*) he'll be kind to you in the future. Instead, you have unwittingly reinforced his letting you down, again, in the future. This is because he is looking for your natural human tendency to really want to expect goodness from him, and when he does provide a kind act, you naturally assume he's changed...and so you're quick to reward that, *because this is what you want from him.*

Please understand that THAT is what *he* wants from *you.* He wants to make sure that you're still emotionally connected to him. If you emotionally react with glee, with a smile, or with a heartfelt thanks, you are telling him that you are still *there.* He can affect you; he can bring you down or bring you up. It's his call. What you are actually reinforcing, therefore, is his assurance that he can manipulate your feelings. And his having disappointed you just before that—*that* will be forgiven and forgotten. All you want is for him to respect you, treat you with some consideration, and be helpful—scratch your back, and you scratch his. That's all you want. But that is not what *he* wants. He wants you on the hook, and your showing emotional gratitude will assure him that you are definitely still prime bait for him.

Therefore, beyond a polite verbal acknowledgment and appreciation of a good deed from him, there is nothing—no emotion, no emotional backing to your politely saying, "Thanks, Ted. I really appreciate that. Makes the day go easier." This is a dispassionate acknowledgment of the instance of his cooperating with you in the course of the teamwork process of the day. This is businesslike, matter-of-fact, and devoid of emotion.

The most effective thing you can do with a person whom you can't trust (but must be in the same environment with, day after day) is to become emotionally neutral, to respond politely with an emotionally unaffected mental state. Wouldn't that show the distrusted coworker you're on to him? That you're done with getting disappointed, betrayed, let down, and hurt? That you've essentially removed yourself from that person? Disconnected, disengaged, unaffected?

Removing your emotions—to the point where you're emotionally *freezing that person out*. Isn't that what you'd wind up doing? Is it not sad to be in a situation where you simply can't afford to be yourself, can't afford to let your guard down, can't extend true warmth (called "warm fuzzies" in the '70s), and can't be sincerely friendly? You can't be yourself because being yourself, being emotionally reachable and engaging with your own style and charm, will mean something to him that most people most of the time don't bother thinking about. It will mean that you are acknowledging his presence, accepting him as an emotional being in your immediate area. You are acknowledging his existence on an emotional level, which is the basic nature of human beings. We crave this like we crave air. (You wouldn't want to be frozen out like that, would you? So doesn't it occur to you that the other person is counting on (consciously or not) precisely that, which would *empathically* stop you from going there?)

Yes, this is sad, to have to remove your unique self from the moment. But if done consistently with your coworker, he might get the point: **you want him to respect you.** This situation forces you into not wanting that person to like you, not wanting that person to love you, but wanting that person to *respect* you. You are no longer even *interested* in him liking or loving you. It's gotten way beyond that point. His emotions no longer matter to you. And by freezing that person out, by removing yourself from him, that—and only that—might lead him into realizing that you're no longer available to kick around anymore. It might lead him to realize that you've learned your lesson: being emotionally available only causes you hurt and disappointment.

Now, there's a good chance that this might work with your coworker. But your coworker doesn't really need you, doesn't have to rely on you, and really has no true stake in respecting you and regaining your trust. (He's got gas in his own car, y'know?)

But your child *does*. In reality, you *are* in the position to reempower yourself. Your child, who needs you, *does* have a real stake in respecting you and regaining your trust. You provide the basics for your child, don't you? Take dinner, for example. Not only do you provide the kitchen, the table, the chair, and utensils, but you also provide the food. And then there's the Nike shoes, the designer clothes, the iPod, and the cell phone. How would your child *get* these things if it weren't for you?

> The reality is, you would have a much better chance of finally getting respect from the child you don't trust than from the coworker you don't trust.

Some parents find this easy to grasp, but most do not. Most parents—usually Mom—find it appalling. When I tell that mother to remove the escape clause from her contract with her son, I am specifically addressing this always overlooked strategy that is available to her—to emotionally freeze her child out. But no matter how emotionally devastated that mother is, no matter how much hurt her son or daughter has inflicted on her, she will ***not*** do it. Will *not* consider it. Impossible. The extent to which we humans refuse to emotionally freeze another person out is truly amazing. And if that other person happens to be our child? Wow. It's absolutely unthinkable. *Instead, the parent will remain emotionally available to the child, which is the **ultimate** escape clause— that which nullifies the contract.*

But in the case of the disempowered parent, this strategy is absolutely necessary. And it is the ONE THING that the parent has not tried—*will* not try—in order to regain the proper relationship with the child. She will most likely walk out of my office, seek help elsewhere, and once again proclaim, "I've tried *every*thing and nothing works with my son!"

Really? She's tried everything?

Let's say her daughter, Amber, kicks the cat, throws a fit at Walmart, and forces Mom to buy a toy, and then she blames Mom that the toy isn't what she really wanted, yelling and demanding to return to Walmart for a different toy. She is now lying on her back, pounding her feet on the floor, and screeching and cursing her mom. What to do? Ah, a time-out. That'll do it. Mom tells Amber to go to her room for a time-out, which might require dragging Amber into her room and shutting (locking?) her door. Mom will then hear even louder screaming and cursing, some banging and throwing stuff. (I had one five-year-old who threw a chair through an Andersen vinyl window.) Mom will definitely hear Amber shout, "You're mean!" (If she does, I tell Mom, you're actually doing a good job. Hearing "you're mean" is an A on the parenting report card.) But if a time-out was part of the contract—that if Amber kicks the cat and throws a scene in the store, she will get a time-out—how is that being *mean*? Timing out is a way of calming down, regrouping, reassessing, and having the time to reflect on what just occurred and to understand how another person might be feeling. Mom's contract with Amber includes the *purpose* of the time-out, which should produce a contrite, perhaps meek child, eager to make amends, to set things right. That's the contract.

After an hour or so, Amber grows weary. Mom hears only silence. A bit later, Amber quietly opens her door and seeks out Mom, who is sitting on the sofa. With glee and with a picture she'd colored in her hand, she leaps onto Mom's lap and happily shows her what she's done. Gosh, ain't that swell? Amber's in a good mood. She's treating Mom very well! Wow. Isn't this valuable? Shouldn't this be rewarded and positively reinforced?

Maybe B. F. Skinner would agree: if Amber is treating Mom well, this should be reinforced. So, typically—most moms report this, and I shudder when they do—Mom will respond with equal glee, spewing forth warm fuzzies in response to Amber's sudden reversal into good behavior. *(What contract?)*

What Mom is really telling Amber is that the behavior occurring *before* the good behavior is FREE, that it hasn't caused her mother to have some mixed feelings about Amber, and that

The Tyranny of Unconditional Love

it hasn't really hurt her mother's feelings. Everything's fine! *(Unwittingly, Mom is positively reinforcing Amber's tantrum.)* The reason for Amber's switch into good behavior was to get the crucial reassurance that what she did earlier didn't change how Mom feels about her. (A pure ADHD child can't do this.)

> Please understand that Amber is not different from other children. Your child will give you the dilemma of deeply hurting you *and* using your unconditional love for her as an escape from the contract the two of you agreed on.

Mom still loves Amber. Unconditionally. And she communicates this by remaining emotionally present to her throughout this vignette. The sequence—an angry, defiant Amber leads to angry Mom leads to Amber reversing her attitude leads to Mom also reversing *her* attitude—this tells Amber that Mom is emotionally available to her and is acknowledging her presence, her emotions, and her existence. It gives Amber the powerful message that Mom's feelings for Amber are not conditional upon how Amber treats her. Mom is still there for Amber to treat her however she wants. The contract is voided.

Unconditional love. Isn't that what you'd like to always have for your child? Wonderful, isn't it?

Yes, it is wonderful. To unconditionally love your child forever and ever and ever. And ever. Two years, eight years, thirteen years. Gosh, I'm getting teary here.

But loving Amber unconditionally at that moment does the exact opposite of what Mom *should* be doing for her child. The reason for this is that Amber will interpret that unconditional love as including unconditional trust and unconditional positive regard for her. Unwittingly, Mom reassures Amber that everything is okay, that no matter what Amber does, Mom not only still loves her but trusts her as well. Amber gets the crucial reassurance that no matter how she behaves, it won't change how her mother feels about her, and it won't cause her mother to emotionally *leave* her.

In effect, her mother is lying to her, because feelings toward your child really *do* change when you're treated like this. I know you try hard to deny it, and your stubborn persistence in trying to maintain unconditional love for your child is *why* you try hard to deny it.

The irony of this is that you—like most parents—actually do change from unconditionally loving at least one of your child's behaviors to loving that behavior conditionally (where there is no escape clause).

Toilet Training

Let's look at an example of unconditional love turning into conditional love—that is, unconditional positive regard for your child becoming positive regard for your child **on the condition** that she changes her behavior and does what you want her to do. This example, of course, assumes that you in fact started out with unconditional love for this behavior. Some parents don't, but most do, usually with their very first newborn just home from the hospital. The room is decorated with plenty of baby stuff all around, those many outward signs showing your natural and heartfelt unconditional love for your child. Many parents behold their first child's first poop as a wonderful product, with unconditional acceptance of the poop. Some remark that it's adorable, while others wonder about the color, the amount, and so forth. Having to deal with shit is met with admiration, as well as with unconditional love, which, remember, the child automatically assumes includes unconditional positive regard.

This goes on for a while. Many parents—even dads!—view diaper changing as part of the deal, unconditionally accepting this as part of life. This is what you signed up for. There's no question, nothing to quibble about (except, maybe, who gets to change the next diaper), and it normally, usually, and reasonably doesn't in any way affect how you feel about your child.

But when poop as a wonderful product becomes poop as a smelly, inconvenient product, unconditional acceptance of it begins to wane, doesn't it? It is said that "normal" potty training can take up to five years, but many parents begin to look forward to that awesome day, when the child delays a bowel movement until securely atop the toilet, as early as year two. If your child persists in needing you to deal with her poop into the third or fourth year, your attitude begins to change, doesn't it? Many parents adopt a potty training exercise for their child, diligently helping her to master the small steps needed to succeed at eliminating the need for diapers. It is during this process that you, whether you know it or not, change from unconditional acceptance of all of your child's behaviors to conditional acceptance of at least one behavior. You don't want to deal with her shit anymore, and you let her know it.

"I'll clean up your awesome shit" becomes "I don't want to deal with your shit anymore." And this evolution of your regard for your child is, really, a win-win situation. You don't have to change diapers anymore; your child doesn't need someone to clean him up anymore. In most cases, this gets to the point where your child doesn't *want* anyone to clean her up anymore.

Please think about this. "Tommy doesn't need someone to clean him up anymore" is really "Tommy needs *no one* to clean him up anymore." Your child's need has changed from needing to depend on others to needing to do for himself. What's fascinating about this is that although your child started out *needing* to be cleaned up, he didn't start out consciously *wanting* to be cleaned up. Your evolution from total unconditional love to partially conditional love paralleled your child's evolving from needing his diaper changed to *needing and wanting* to take adequate care of himself. Simply put, he no longer wants you to deal with his shit anymore.

> Once your child masters toilet training, he no longer expects you to deal with it. In fact, he actually welcomes your conditional love when it is met with his readiness to mature.

Now, can you imagine what might happen if you continued with unconditional positive regard and love for him and his soiled diapers? If you didn't guide him in toilet training with subtle, positive responses for using the toilet and subtle, negative (or neutral) responses while changing his diaper—what do you think would happen if you continued with unconditional positive regard toward him soiling himself? We can imagine that the concept of not expecting you to change his diaper would never start occurring to him. He would then proceed with an expectation that you *would* clean up his poop. He would continue soiling himself without knowing that he's supposed to clean up his own mess, and he wouldn't have a clue that he is *not* supposed to have the expectation that you will clean it up.

Is that fair to him? Is allowing him the false notion that you will continue to clean up his mess and not mind doing so fair to him?

Is carrying on like that, with the pressure of being expected to go on and on and on changing your child's diapers, fair to you?

In a sense, we can imagine that this might be fair to both of you. It's the status quo, and you're both used to it. One mother blatantly told me, "I admit that in a sense…I miss it. Like, my daughter doesn't need me anymore or, or something. She's already starting to grow up!" As time goes by, it will get increasingly harder to change this situation. So you both might languish in the status quo, colluding to keep it going. (There are some women who do this with breast-feeding, but that's another story.)

Imagine that your child is staying over at your folks' place or that a babysitter is subbing for you. It could go both ways: your child—if he's smart enough—might intuit that other people would not fancy changing his diaper when he's six years old. *Or*—if he's not that brilliant—he might not intuit this and might expect others to change it. Hence, two possible scenarios: he expects only *you* to change his diaper (mysteriously able not to expect others to do so), or he expects *everyone* to change it.

Many children behave quite well in my office. Without exception, the mother will not understand it. "I have no idea why she's behaving like this today. This isn't normal!" (Interesting choice of words there: *normal*.) Then Mom will explain that her child seems to give only *her* a problem. Around others, the child obeys, she's respectful, and she's polite…

Does this ring true with you? Most of the conduct-disordered children I see for the first time act appropriately in my office, while Mom tells me about all their aggressive, destructive behaviors and hostile attitudes. In response to Mom's bewilderment about this, I tell her *why* and *how* her child is able to behave that way. She will actually ask, "Then why?" And I respond, "Because she *can*, that's why. She is able to make the choice to behave in my office. *How* she does that is by correctly intuiting the fact that I won't put up with any nonsense. Somehow, she manages to take me seriously." (Some moms get *really* angry at this.)

Now let's explore the toilet training analogy further. Let's say your child expects only *you* to change her diaper. This is a statement of your relationship with her and her knowledge that this is okay with you. It's about your relationship with your child and what you taught her to expect from you. It's a tango, taking two. Do you realize that consciously or subconsciously, she assumes that you *need* her to expect you to change her diaper, and that if she didn't, she'd somehow be letting you down?

The depth of the collusion between you and your child is awesome. Much of it goes unnoticed by both of you, which makes it largely subconscious. But it's a dance that you must do together, because in part, it defines your relationship. It defines your child's self-image as well as yours. In this scenario, your child is able to toilet herself when she's around others, but she soils herself when she's around you. This means that she *can* clean up her own shit. She does not expect others to do it. But around you, she *can't* clean up her mess, because it doesn't jibe with the nature of your relationship with her. She's not deliberately victimizing you, even if you yell at her for soiling herself and she yells back, calling you names and hurting your feelings. She's not that way as a sole agent. She's that way because subconsciously, you both *expect* this ordeal to carry on. After all, didn't you choose to continually unconditionally love her even though she failed to potty train? Not only does she assume that this is the norm, but she also thinks that you expect it.

Remember, back in Chapter 3, how a child was repeatedly throwing toys around the room and running amok, disturbing other clients, while Mom was trying to have a conversation with someone else. I've watched many moms with their children in waiting rooms. I've seen—and so have you—Mom repeatedly say, "Stop it! What did I tell you?" Again and again. Once in my office, she'll say (with a smile), "Oh, he's a handful!"

He's a *handful?* I wonder. He is a handful and will continue being a handful because mom subconsciously *likes* his being a handful. "Ornery" is another overused word, and her smiling while gushing out that euphemism tells him this awful truth. He *knows* that Mom doesn't really expect him to mind her. At some level—and this is deep, I realize—he knows that Mom *needs* him to ignore her. Why? Because this is part of her self-image or her job security, if you will. **This is her needing to be needed to continually reprimand her son.** *This* makes her a mom—a person, someone worthwhile, important, and useful. It is this fulfilled need that produces her smile when she calls him "a handful."

My point here is this: if your child behaves well around others but not around you—as he might expect you and not his grandmother to change his diaper—it's a function of your relationship with him. In this case (your child being smart enough to comport properly with others) your child, in a sense, is growing himself up. *He* has determined that diaper-soiling and diaper-changing at the age of six is a complete no-no when around others. Smart kid. He knows what the world expects of him, despite your coddling of his continued soiling.

The Tyranny of Unconditional Love

A less-gifted child won't know this. She will act the same around others as she does around you, whether it's soiling or misbehaving. The bigger problem here is that she thinks the world resembles you — that everyone will expect what you expect of her. She merely doesn't have the extra intellectual oomph to intuit the issue. (Higher intelligence usually helps the child mature, no matter what you do.)

In short, we can appreciate the natural, automatic change from unconditional love to conditional love when toilet training is to be learned and mastered. Using this example, we can extrapolate to other issues your child must learn and master. Just as you are invested in changing unconditional love to conditional love in order to help your child achieve toilet training, so too are you invested in changing unconditional love to conditional love in order to help your child achieve other skills necessary for immersion in our world.

> Therefore, we can see that persisting with unconditionally loving your child becomes counterproductive in helping your child become socially acceptable.

You've evolved from willingly cleaning up shit to refusing to deal with shit. If your child achieved toilet training, you've already made the shift from unconditional positive regard to conditional positive regard — rewarding certain behaviors and extinguishing other behaviors. In order to have accomplished this, you had to truly be interested in your child's emotional and social growth.

CHAPTER 8

SUSPENDING YOUR LOVE

Your child's emotional and social maturation equates with her understanding and accepting that the world does not unconditionally love us. This understanding involves not only attracting love and other positive emotions, but also attracting and obtaining fondness, esteem, attention, and acknowledgment as well as being valued. In early childhood, we get these things because we simply exist. We don't have to do anything to get attention or acknowledgment. We are indeed precious. Within the framework of our homes and our families, we matter simply because we are there. We don't have to do anything to earn esteem from others, and we are acting our age. We can even shit in our pants, and we're still loved. We don't have to clean up our own shit in order for people to accept and acknowledge us.

But as we get a little bit older, as the potty training discussion shows us, we begin to learn that people will accept us much more readily if we start to clean up after ourselves. (That's after a bowel movement *and* after we're done eating. Could this also apply to cleaning our rooms?) And we gradually learn that we get love, warm fuzzies, and positive reinforcement when we earn them. Positive regard is not unconditional. It's conditional—conditional upon how we behave, how we perform, and how we treat others. Moreover, it is our parents who provide these lessons about trust, mistrust, autonomy, shame, doubt, guilt, conformity, rebellion, assertiveness, intimacy, isolation, industriousness, and inferiority—so that we learn what the world will find worthy about us and what we have to do in order to earn this regard. It is the job of parents to teach children how to behave in order to be accepted, acknowledged, valued, and respected.

So I ask you this: how late do you want to delay letting your child in on the truth? Would you deny the nonexistence of Santa Claus once your son or daughter firmly insists he doesn't exist? Your role as parent is to teach your child about the world. Surely you understand your child's need to evolve into knowing that Santa doesn't exist—just as you understand her need to evolve into self-toileting. Can you also understand that your role as parent is to not delude your child into thinking other unreal things about our world? So why would you allow Amber to assume that the Walmart tantrum, kicking the cat, and verbally mistreating you are all okay with you? Wouldn't that grow her into a person who might assume that the rest of the world is just like you, too?

Hence, Mom's only valid parental response—in her role as world representative—when Amber leaps onto her lap is to gently remove Amber from her lap, look deeply into her eyes, and softly say, "Amber, I am not ready for this. You need to leave me alone now." Then Amber's mother gets up from the sofa and slowly walks away. If Amber follows into her personal space, Mom should gently place Amber at a distance from her and firmly insist that she be left alone. Mom might mention the truth that she feels hurt, disappointed, betrayed, and let down by Amber's prior behavior and attitude. That is to be dwelled on. After all, Amber had a point to make, didn't she? She wanted to be impressive (in a negative way), right? So don't disappoint *her*. You can show her that, yes, she did make an impression on you, and you got the point. If you must show her any feeling, showing her sadness—*not* anger—is essential at this point. Sadness is your real, bottom-line emotion at this point, the essence of your internal state. Showing anger—which, of course, is tearing at you—is not a *bad* idea, but it invites an engagement, a quarrel, and an exchange. And in order to really make *your* point, you must show her that you're done. You understand where she's coming from, and you need no further confirmation from her. She did a good job with making you grasp her position. And revealing your sadness is the best acknowledgment you can give her at that moment. Most of all, you quietly reject her suddenly warm, polite gambit. You do not engage. You are cold. Dispassionate. **This is the emotional ten-foot pole.** This is the core of your strategy to re-empower yourself, improve your relationship with your daughter, regain her respect, and model the world's response to games of manipulation. This is for her, not for you. You're not trying to get revenge or be spiteful here. You are showing her that you've finally *accepted* the fact that emotionally engaging and negotiating with her brings both of you only misery and that it does nothing to help her improve her knowledge of how to be acceptable to our world.

Now, I deeply realize that at this juncture, a bystander might scoff at you and deride you for rejecting your daughter and rejecting her precisely at the point where—the other books teach us—you should be doing anything *but* rejecting her. "Why would you reject your daughter when she's treating you nicely?" they'd ask.

If you latch onto that notion, you are sorely missing the point. The notion that you should *not* reject your daughter at that point is the escape clause that is built into all the theories and strategies you've been told. The escape clause insists that, when all is said and done, you still love your daughter. You will acknowledge her, and you will not shun her. You will accept her as an emotional person with whom you choose to negotiate and engage. After all, she's your daughter! After all, you're her mom! BOOM! You accept Amber's leaping onto your lap, and you've escaped. And you took her right with you.

You've escaped, scampered away from your task and from your job of parenting. The point here is *not* to focus on whether or not you love Amber. That entire syrupy mess has no place here, and suspending it might be the only sane thing you can do, because the issue of love deflects from what it is you need to do *for her*. Within the Amber example here, what you need to do is reflect back to her that how she treated you only minutes *before* is not acceptable. Not to you. Not to the world. I understand that it's a shame and a real pain in the ass that being nice right back at her—at this crucial point—is something you can't afford to do, right here, right now. It's a pain in the ass because it goes against everything you've felt and learned about parenting, about reward and punishment, and about disciplining strategies. It feels counterintuitive not to reinforce Amber's good mood at that point.

But the reality is that there is no way that Amber will not perceive your being nice right back at her, at that exact moment, as the signal that what she did moments before is, really, fine with you. It's all okay now because Amber quickly made it all better.

If you be nice at that moment, Amber will see that you're easily swayed, a yo-yo. Either you've got a very bad short-term memory, or you're a pushover. She might not know that she knows this, but she does.

And actually, you're neither one of those. You're simply avoiding the job of parenting your child. You're using the escape clause to negate the contract you made with your child. I say that because the purpose of the contract was to get your child to respect you, to be civil, and to work *with* you in making your household—your personal world—work. Now, how does showing your child how bad your memory is or showing your child how much of a sap you are, how does *that* allow your child to learn to respect you?

Your understanding this is vital. The only emotions you can afford to show your child in this situation are sadness, disappointment, and the feeling of being let down. These are the real feelings, the ones underlying and causing your anger and the need to argue with him. There is nothing more to provide your child at this point. Your child gets nothing else from you, and it is important for you to understand that it will be some time before he *will* get anything else from you, all of which is the essence of the emotional ten-foot pole. You remove yourself from your child, and you hold that position until it sinks in: *Your child will not have you to abuse any longer. You will not negotiate with him.*

It's sad when you can't give those warm fuzzies or when you can't positively reinforce your child. In fact, this is so sad, so cruel, and so unthinkable that you've never been taught to do this before now. It goes against the human spirit. This is your child, yet you reject his smile, warmth, or offer of a hug? How could you! Are you a cold sociopath? An antisocial sadist?

No. You're not. You're actually trying to prevent your child from becoming a sociopath. You're trying to teach him the nature and the value of human relationships. And things have become so awful in your household that the concept of love is just not working. It's as if it's shoved aside, suspended in the midst of interpersonal strife and anguish.

"How did this come to be?" you might ask. "How did things get to this point?" Why did you collude with your child in forsaking the joy of the parent-child relationship, only to choose an atmosphere of distrust, fear, intimidation, power struggles, hostility, and sadness? Why did you not parent your child?

Well, your decision to opt out of parenting was not completely self-willed. As with many parents I've met, you avoided disciplining your child because of traumatic events that occurred in your own childhood and because of your caustic relationship with your own parents. I know that. As a psychiatrist, I know that you haven't parented your child because of very deep scars you've carried from your own youth. (Another book?)

But back to our topic. When I advise Mom to react in this cold fashion, typically, she will react with umbrage, and she'll get angry with me. How can I possibly say this stuff? What kind of a shrink am I? Nuh-uh, not gonna do it, she'll insist. When I remind her of the distrusted coworker analogy, she informs me that she's no fool, and that of course she'd emotionally freeze that person out.

But not her child.

At that point, I might feel obligated to provide some medication for her child, to help the kid better tolerate frustration and disappointment and whatever ineffective discipline the parent continues to offer.

Return to see me in two weeks, I'll say, inwardly throwing up my hands, imagining the jungle existing in that family's household.

CHAPTER 9

IT'S NONNEGOTIABLE

But there are some parents who *do* hear my advice. A few moms have admitted their abdication of the role of parent, who've embraced the concept of the true task of parenting, and who have turned it all around and presented a real model of our world. They understand that the saying, "You scratch my back; I'll scratch yours," applies to their relationship with their children. You cooperate with me; I'll cooperate with you. You give me a problem; I'll give you a problem. (If you obey the speed limit, keep your license. If you repeatedly offend, lose your license.)

If your child makes a bad choice, say, not to clean his room, that particular refusal is not worth arguing about. It's what that choice *represents*: choosing not to cooperate with you and giving you a hard time. In order to effectively expose him to the consequence of his choice, you must respond *in kind* after you observe the choice he's made. (The trick here is the timing of that consequence. You don't knee-jerk a retaliation as a one-up; rather, you allow something relevant to naturally unfold to your child.) If your child chooses not to take out the garbage, then *you* choose not to provide the ice cream. If your child chooses to constantly misbehave, to constantly give you attitude and behavior problems — to the point where you're taking your child to see *me* — then your child is *choosing* not to receive, say, a birthday present, or, God forbid, Christmas presents. (You'd save money here, you know.)

I've asked some parents, "Now that it's three weeks till Christmas, has Brandon been behaving this way — hitting you, punching holes in walls, breaking toys, scaring animals — for the past few months?" The answer is a resounding "Yes!" Then I wonder aloud, "So, I assume, given this behavior, that Brandon will not get any Christmas presents, correct? Y'know, like, he's not really been earning them. Even Santa has a list and checks it twice, right?"

Well! Talk about the eight-hundred-pound gorilla in the room! The parents will grow extremely uneasy with this. Brandon — also present in my office — will clamber onto Mom's lap, ask if they're going to Mickey D's afterward, and try to deflect from the issue and receive the reassurance that his mother's unconditional love will give him. (This is spectacularly irksome as I watch Mom allow him to remain on her lap. Erecting an emotional ten-foot pole is the farthest thing from her mind — because it is completely counterintuitive for her to even imagine. And it is **precisely at this moment** that she should begin to re-empower herself. His behaviors and attitude do *not* merit physical contact and reassurance that everything is okay. Mom's message at that moment must include limit-setting: "We're not here to prove our love to each other now; please get off my lap.") But the mere mention of omitting Christmas suddenly makes Brandon the victim, and mother's nurturing, protective nature will win the moment. (This is a fantastic example of unconditional love making that mom an ineffective, inaccurate parent.)

I then try to lower the room's tension. "Well, he *does* have three weeks left to prove that he really wants Christmas presents, y'know. Whaddaya say, Brandon?"

And with that, silence fills the room. Everyone in that room knows that Brandon will get Christmas presents, and he will get them, by God, no matter how he behaves from now until Christmas. The certainty with which everyone, especially Brandon, knows this is one of the scariest things I run into as a psychiatrist. Brandon has a smug certainty about this, as he remains on Mother's lap; his parents have an apprehensive certainty about it. On Brandon's side, he is smug in the knowledge that he is protected from the reality of the world and that his parents provide him with a thick, protective cushion from the reality that I, the shrink, am trying to inject into the room. Theirs is an extremely tight relationship, with very clear rules and boundaries. Brandon *will* have a Christmas, no matter how he behaves. The boundary around that is thick granite! (And there I am, chipping away at it with a plastic scalpel.)

This is an example of the escape clause. I find Christmas to be the most powerful escape clause (birthdays come second—as if Christmas presents will reset the whole game here. *Sure, he can have Christmas; then he'll know we love him and really care about him. We don't want to remain angry and have a cold war in this house.*

On his parents' side, they too are certain. There is nothing Brandon can do that would negate his Christmas. But I can always sense their apprehension, as if they're thinking, "Hmmmm, so taking this to the end zone, there really *is* nothing he could do that would get us to not give him Christmas presents, and he *knows* this. Uh-oh."

Guess what? At January's appointment, Mom informs me that of course Brandon got presents, but she's had to take most of them from him because of continued bad behaviors. Imagine that. Can you imagine that crazy circus of events? I'll bet you can. If you're reading this, you've been there. (To boot, do you think Brandon even *remembers* what he received for Christmas?)

What I'm telling you here is that it is vital for you to keep yourself out of the drama. Once you have made it clear what's expected of your son or daughter, don't behave as if the contract is open for negotiation. It isn't. Your child's refusal to clean up her room is not something you argue with her about or insert yourself into at all. Just observing her choice not to cooperate is all you do. "What goes around comes around," in this case, is this: her not cleaning her room will come back to haunt her. Her choice will be met by your choice. But you think, what if she says, "Fuck you, Bitch!" when I remind her to clean up her room? What do I say? How do I handle that? This is what you say and do. Look her straight in the eye and reply, "Yep. Bitchy is in my repertoire. You noticed." This response says many things: (1) you responded to the fact of the statement (like most people, you're capable of deserving that label); (2) you are not defending yourself; (3) cleaning up her room is not a topic for arguing or negotiating; (4) if she doesn't clean up her room, you really are not affected (if you did argue the point with her, you'd likely clean it up afterward anyway); and (5) cleaning up her room is taking care of herself, cooperating with others, and being responsible. It has *nothing* to do with you.

Brandon's bad choices—not doing chores, for example—are *not* to be argued with. You politely ask him to take out the garbage. You can remind him once or twice, but that's your call. After that, for God's sake, do *not* ask him, "What did I tell you to do, young man?" (It advertises to him that you have a terrible short-term memory.) You do *not* argue with him. You simply **observe** the choice he makes. Does he cooperate with you or not? If he does, then *you* cooperate with *him*, say, by honoring that promise of a movie or ice-skating trip. If he does not cooperate with you, then you don't cooperate with him. "Uh, Brandon, we're out of ice cream, not gonna do a movie." (And please do not use money as an excuse by saying, "We can't afford it." Saying that is being very defensive. You're explaining yourself, using finances as the reason for depriving him of those things. You're copping out, trying to avoid being called "mean." Stay focused. You're trying to parent him, to show him the consequence of his behavior, not the consequence of your cash flow problem.)

Remember, our world is based on the merit system. We don't get paid for simply being our wonderful selves. We get paid when we earn it. Did your child earn those birthday presents, that movie, the dessert, and other extras? (In this context, "earn" = respect you.) I've had mothers walk out of my office in a huff, dragging the child with them, when I broach this issue

The Tyranny of Unconditional Love

with them. And guess what? The child understands the entire issue. When Mom drags him or her out of the office, what do you think that child realizes? That Mom has reinforced the illogical obsession with unconditional love. (And calling me a quack is a great escape clause!) Amber is now even *more* assured that anything she does is free. It really *doesn't* matter to her mom; Amber simply does not have to care about what she does, says, or thinks. Hurting Mom's feelings is allowed. After all, nothing bad will happen. And all this is because Amber intuits that the escape clause—unconditional love—is much more important to her mom than sticking to discipline.

> It is the child's assuredness of precisely this—the existence of the escape clause—that is the exact reason why you have a monster on your hands.

See what we have here? Who does the caring? Certainly not Amber. It's the parent who does all the caring and worrying and self-doubting and fretting. To totally own all the caring not only lets Amber off the hook, but it also does what Pepsi does for our thirst. You know that drinking high fructose corn syrup—the essential ingredient in regular soda pop—actually increases our thirst, right? I'm thirsty, so I drink caffeinated sugar, which briefly quenches my thirst but then actually reinforces my being thirsty. (Sugar and caffeine make us pee.) So by showing that you care so much about your *conflict* with Amber, you are assuring her that you *care* about her, that you *love* her! If your child gets you to engage in an argument about this, she's actually changed the subject. Suddenly, it's about self-esteem, who can argue better, who knows more curse words, who is right, who is wrong, and who is moral and who isn't. It's also about whether you love her or not. That is the escape clause being used by your child. If push comes to shove—if she wins and doesn't do her chores—you still love her.

What? What does doing chores have to do with love? Her doing chores is a parental guide to practicing being responsible and self-accountable. Your job as parent is to do just that—guide her— not to get into a heated discussion about your character, her character, or whether you love her or not.

It is vital that you understand that the expression of *any* feelings in this type of situation implies a certain level of caring. Look, if a stranger dislikes your orange sweater, do you care about that? If your spouse dislikes it, *don't* you care about that? Whether you respond with happiness (let's say your mother-in-law got it for you) or with anger (let's say you treated yourself at Bloomingdale's), you are likely to have more feelings about your spouse disliking it than the stranger disliking it. You might care so little about the stranger disliking it that you don't show any emotion at all. You show neutrality. (Neutral = no feelings one way or the other.) If you are Amber's mother and she gets any emotional response from you—from pure joy to hot rage—she has struck gold. She sees that she affects you, that she influences how you feel. We humans are wired to instinctively want to be able to affect each other. If I change you from feeling nothing to feeling *some*thing, I influence you. If I have influence over you, then I matter to you. (Existentialist philosophers might say it this way: if I matter to you, then I exist.) If you respond emotionally to her under these circumstances, you are telling her that she is still a person with whom you will emotionally negotiate and engage (no ten-foot pole).

> The more you show angry emotions about an issue, the more you advertise how much you *care* about that issue. This assures your child that you love her. Therefore, this increases the chances that your child will perpetuate the conflicted relationship with you. Why not?

The Tyranny of Unconditional Love

Reminder: Never care about the process or content during an argument more than your child does. Your job is to teach your child the value of contributing to the household, not to win an argument about the merits of the chore-system in your house, or whether the label "mean" applies to you. You're not the issue here. Being called mean is not to be avoided. (You're stronger than that.) Your child calling you mean is a manipulation tactic. It's your child who must—beginning as early as eighteen months—evolve into being concerned about how *she* thinks and feels and behaves and about how she treats you.

She must learn to treat you with respect. Isn't that the way our world works? It is the parent who has the privilege of cluing the child in to the workings of our world, isn't it? If Amber doesn't do her chores, or if she hits you, disrespects you, or calls you mean, or if she has fits when told no, that's not the time to reassure her that you care about her and love her by getting all steamed about her defiant attitude or behavior. It's not about you! It's not about whether you're really not mean or whether Amber doesn't get angry with you or whether you're being unfair.

> It's about letting your child know what our world expects from her and how our world is structured. It's about showing her how *she* will be treated if she lacks respect for others.

CHAPTER 10

DON'T JUST DO SOMETHING. OBSERVE.

THE EFFECTIVE PSYCHOTHERAPIST — OR the clinician or counselor — is a "participant-observer." While participating in an interpersonal transaction, the therapist keeps an eye on what's going on during his or her interaction with a client, which means absorbing the *content* of what is being said *and* simultaneously observing the **process** of the interaction while the dialogue is occurring. The purpose of this is to gain more information about the nature of the interaction than would be gathered only from what is spoken by the client. Thus, the therapist gets crucial information about the other person's ***agenda***.

When interacting with your child, you maximize your active parenting by both participating in the interaction and observing your child's agenda. Not only that, but you might also get a notion of your *own* agenda. You will be amazed at what you learn about both your child and yourself if you do this, as well as learning the reasons for the repeated futile arguments you and your child keep having. Most of the time, these arguments are disputes over the content of what we say, such as "Did you clean your room or not," "Am I a bitch or not," or "Is my husband a bastard or not." When I ask the parent and the child, "So, what do you argue about?" and they respond, "Anything and everything!" and then I ask, "Like what?" and they are at a loss to recall any specific examples—you can bet that it's the nitpicky details of some forgotten squabble that hung them up in arguing and berating each other. The original issue, say, to do chores, is put on the back burner. This is a shame, because this moment as an opportunity to parent your child gets lost in a completely different agenda.

<u>Chores</u>

Let's say your son refuses to do some chore. You're probably reluctant even to bring it up. Once you do remind him, he still (predictably) doesn't do it. Then you find yourself arguing with him about doing it. (This is the **content** I referred to earlier.)

The obvious **process** here is the power struggle with your child. Who's gonna win this one? But the *hidden* process is much, much more than that. Underlying the power struggle is your showing your child that you *care* about whether he does the chore, that somehow his not doing the chore affects *you*. (Please, are you really counting on him to relieve you of having to take his dirty dinner dishes to the sink? If you're reading this, I think it's way beyond that.)

Think about it. Does your exceeding the speed limit really bother the state trooper? He really doesn't care if you speed or not. If you speed, he stops you. And when he stops you, he doesn't seem angry, right? (He even tells you to have a nice day.) If you don't speed, he lets you drive. Would you speed *just to affect him?* (If you did, I doubt it would anger him, but it might amuse him.) It's a stretch, isn't it, to think that your speeding will get the best of

The Tyranny of Unconditional Love

him? He's doing his job, but he's not emotionally invested in it so much that he cares more about your driving than you do.

Now, following that analogy, why should your daughter's refusing to take out the garbage get the best of you? Well, it does get the best of you if you wind up yelling at her or back at her, in any way jousting with her and arguing, back and forth, back and forth. The superficial power struggle process is underscored—no, actually *driven*—by the fact that you *care*. (You let it get to you and let it press your buttons.) And what are you spending so much energy and time actually caring about, anyway? The last word? Proving that you're not a bitch, that your IQ is above one hundred, or that you're a moral, fair person?

In order for you to be arguing with her, you must *care* about the issue you're arguing about. In order for any of us to express any emotion, whether it's happy or angry or sad, we must care about it. There has to be an emotional investment, a buy-in. Otherwise, we wouldn't feel any which way about it.

So during the debate about whether to comply, your child is getting a great big treat: he gets tremendous reassurance that you care about him and his part of the argument. *That* is the true—the *real*—agenda. Listen, the police officer cares about me in terms of my driving. If my driving endangers society, the officer attends to me. (I've yet to be stopped by a cop for safe driving and be rewarded. Unless I speed, the officer ignores me.) It's the officer's job—this should sound familiar to you by now—to help me (and my driving) be acceptable to our world. If I try to argue with the officer about my driving speed, he or she immediately recognizes the process—that is, my agenda—and shows absolutely *no* caring about me, my agenda, or my feelings.

In the heat of arguing with your son about doing the chore, you wind up caring about the situation more than your son does. *That* is one of the biggest mistakes that you, as a parent, can make. Think about it. Will it be your job to care more about his paying his taxes than he does? Unless you want to keep the umbilical cord intact, don't you want him to care enough about his own welfare that you don't have to? (If he thinks you do care more about his taxes than he does, he might ask for your credit card.)

So doing the chore is his deal. You have nothing to do with it. (I suspect you're still thinking about the chore needing to be done, and I'll get to that.) Whether he obeys you or not, whether he does the chore with a bad attitude or not, it doesn't affect you. It has to affect him. Doing that chore is important for him, important for him to gain your trust, to learn the value of cooperation, and to understand that the world he's heading into demands reciprocity. This is far removed from whether he obeys you or not to see who's in control, or to spite you, to assert power over you, to make you feel bad, or to prove that you really are a vile, mean idiot. If you engage in these content topics with him, you're following his lead to deflect onto issues that are totally irrelevant to the task at hand. This usually happens because you're emotionally involved with those topics. Your self-esteem is pinned to the actual words he uses, and he will pounce on any Achilles heel he knows you have. (In other words, you let your buttons get pushed.) Without an emotional ten-foot pole, you are putty in his hands!

I recently saw a father who was profoundly depressed because his sixteen-year-old daughter, Shania, continually put him down for being unavailable to her during part of her junior year in high school. He'd become addicted to opiates (pain pills) after starting to abuse the Vicodin scripts his orthopedic surgeon prescribed. Once it affected his job (as well as his family), his boss insisted he go out of state to a ninety-day rehab program in order to avoid getting fired. During his time away, he missed out on Shania's prom and much of the decision process about which colleges she should apply to. Not only was he feeling shame about the effects his addiction had had on her and the rest of the family, but he also felt very guilty about not being there for his daughter.

Well, rather than come to him with the depression and feelings of being let down by her dad, Shania chose to verbally assault him with her (reasonable) anger, but she took it to the extreme and actually developed an oppositional defiant disorder (ODD). Nothing he could do or say would get her to forgive him and let him off the hook, no matter how sincerely he apologized and showed true remorse for his mistakes. To her, he was *persona non grata* as well as completely unacceptable to her as a father. Unfortunately, Shania made the decision, whether consciously or not, to go way beyond her reasonable, justified, and entitled anger, and she began to milk her dad's guilt and shame for all she could. Discipline, setting limits, and cooperation became a joke. She funneled her anger through an entitled assumption that his mistake somehow relieved her of daily responsibilities at home. At first, he felt compelled to be lenient and forgiving with her, allowing limits and rules to be bent and, finally, broken. This led to her acting out her anger through using drugs, skipping school, and ultimately to physically assaulting her dad. This then resulted in Shania's fabricating an incident of child abuse and actually calling the Department of Human Services, claiming that he was assaulting *her*, all in response to his trying to wrest things around and regain some parental empowerment over her persisting refusal to do her *chores*.

The problem with all of this is that it wasn't just Shania's will to develop oppositional defiant disorder. Her father had, actually, begun the whole process by allowing his guilt to interfere with his holding on to his parental status and continuing to discipline her *in spite of* the mistakes he had made and the betrayal he had committed. His self-esteem had become pinned to what she thought and felt about him, once he'd made those huge mistakes. He allowed himself to become passionate and defensive about how she felt about him, rather than maintaining the healthy emotional distance often required in the role of parent. He had no emotional ten-foot pole. When she said to him, "You're nothing but a druggie, Dad! You're worthless to me!" she couldn't have hit closer to the mark. He knew it. She knew it. He might've begun turning the whole thing around if he'd merely replied, "I know all that. You sure don't hold any punches, honey. You nailed it, and I *am* very sorry." This acknowledgment would have defused much of the heated emotion, because it is straightforward and not defensive, and it's real. He can be sorry about his mistake and still properly parent his child.

See, doing the "Let's see who's gonna give in" dance—which is really the "Let's see who cares about this more" dance—is

Dad's agenda trying to match hers in a power play, in order to see whose ego is bigger and who can win the battle. In this particular vignette, Shania and Dad struggled to gain the upper hand, her father unwittingly giving in to the idea that his mistake somehow removed her domestic obligations. Shania used the "It's my way or the highway" game, which is a contest of wills that can be played both ways, and doing it can suggest to your child that the world is necessarily a contentious place. See, the child thinks that doing the chore is just to shut you up and that feeling good means *not doing the chore*. (In this case, defying her father passively released her anger, which helped her feel vindicated, and therefore better, by getting her way.) By the end of the tug-of-war, you and your child are far removed from the lesson she needs to learn. Instead of using the chore as an example of mutual help and reciprocity, of cooperation and trust-building, the **process** disintegrates into a meaningless battle of wills: you against your child.

> The real kicker here is that the whole process would never have happened unless there was the initial assumption that doing the chore is optional, that doing the chore is just your capricious whim, or that the chore is arbitrary.
>
> Gosh, is earning a paycheck by doing your job description arbitrary?

I'm asking that you, by erecting an emotional ten-foot pole, step away from the temptation to spar with your child. Given an initial assumption that chores are not optional and that your asking for help is not whimsical, you've already assigned a certain chore for your son or your daughter to do. Megan clears the dinner table; Tucker loads the dishwasher. If they "forget" this, okay, remind them once or twice; it's your call. But after that, step away from the issue and *observe* the choices your children make, not whether they do as they're told, but whether they cooperate with you or not. *This act of calmly observing is part of your dispassionate ten-foot pole.*

If Megan clears the table, she is choosing to cooperate. If Tucker doesn't load the washer, he's choosing not to cooperate. *Neither act should make you second-guess yourself about the chores you assigned to them.*

But what, you ask, do you then do with Tucker? What about the chore not getting done? A glance might be sufficient, your face registering disappointment, a letdown feeling, or betrayal. You might admit it verbally: "Hey Tucker, I thought we had a deal, the three of us. Something we agreed on." And the truth, "I feel let down right now." **And you shut up and let him be.** Leave him with the choice he made. At that point, your silence speaks volumes. You might notice his trying to subtly warm up to you, either physically or emotionally — perhaps right then, or perhaps days later. Please look for that. It's his way of assuring himself that you unconditionally love him. Do not bite. Don't reciprocate. Brush him off with, "Tuck, please leave me alone now. I'm done for now," spoken softly, sadly, and perhaps with a sigh. *I will no longer emotionally negotiate with you. And I'm not sure when I will choose to be ready to do so. Just because you want to nicely emote to me right now, it doesn't knee-jerk me into engaging with you on any emotional level.* (It is very important for you to understand that, yes, your child might withhold emotional attention from you for days. If you feel you're not ready to emotionally respond and remove the pole, then don't. This is something you must feel in your gut.)

That's it. At that point you shut up — *especially* if he has a smart response to your being real and communicating your true feelings — and you quietly load the dishwasher. (If you're going to wind up loading it anyway, judging from his past lack of cooperation, it's better to be doing it quietly, not angrily.) Doing this will send a huge message to everyone in the household: Tucker is not reliable, not to be trusted. He will let you down. (His smart response to your telling him you feel let down might be, "What about all the times YOU let ME down? To which you calmly reply, "Then you know how it feels.")

And you remember the choice he made. He chose not to cooperate with you. He gave you a problem. He let you down. If he chooses to do this and verbally disrespects you at the same time, please don't disrespect him back. Do not become arrogant to top his arrogance. Big mistake.

The "punishment" he gets for not loading the dishwasher is a subtle one, but one that will teach him about how our world works. His punishment is knowing — and believe me, he knows — that he's lost some of your trust, that he's affected how you feel about him. He has disabled himself as a person you will emotionally engage with, which is a powerful message. You will be helping him internalize the need to do his chore for himself, not for you, and that *his* sense of well-being will be compromised if he disappoints you, not *your* sense of well-being. If he wants you to emotionally engage and negotiate with him — to treat him as a living, significant other — he must regain your trust in order for you to remove the pole. (You might be thinking here, "Would I *ever* remove it?" If you are, good for you!)

This is what our world is all about. It's the job — and why not the joy? — of parenting, **to teach your child how our world works and how to be an effective part of it.**

Let's get more positive here. Imagine that you've just asked ten-year-old Tucker to load the dishwasher, and he doesn't want to do it. (I doubt many of us look forward to loading the damn thing.) So, what if...*what if he says to you*, "Y'know, Mom, I don't wanna do that. Right now I'm tired. I really don't." Imagine that he says this politely, showing the weariness and fatigue he's reporting and not masking it with a bad attitude. Further imagine that he appears sincere, that you and he relate to one another with mutual respect and trust. Should this happen, consider yourself lucky. *This* is about mutual cooperation. He is not being disrespectful to you, nor is he using your asking him to do something as an opportunity to visit another agenda. He is not *changing* the agenda of responding to your request to an agenda of getting into a power struggle with you, and he's not using his response to you in such a way that you may doubt if you can trust him. He is responding to your request, and he gives you a reason why he'd rather not cooperate with you at this time.

This is straightforward negotiating about the task of your household at this time, which might be, say, to get the dishes out of the way so as to proceed to some evening's activity; it could be homework, watching a movie together, or a basketball game. Of course you're observing that he's not loading the dishwasher, and you're empathic because you know what it's like to be tired when asked to do something. So your response to Tucker is, "Okay, Tuck, that's reasonable and honest. ," followed with something like, "I'll load up, and you start the movie." This is not a power struggle. No one is keeping score here, and there's no other agenda creeping in and getting in the way of your household (your world) accomplishing the tasks of the evening. In this normal relationship, you and your son enjoy a mutually respectful and cooperative relationship that will "hold" the contingency that Tucker might very well beg off from loading the dishwasher again tomorrow night. You're okay with that, because there is mutual trust here. (Note two things. First, don't make a big deal about your giving him some slack here. Don't make the mistake of warily saying something like, "Yeah, Tucker, but tomorrow night you'd better load the damn washer *and* you'll also get to scrub the floor." This represents your paranoia that just because you give him an inch today, he'll likely want a mile tomorrow. Doing this might give your child a reasonable complaint about you, that *you* started the whole distrust thing going. And you *might* have first done something like this months ago, now finding yourself—to your bewildered dismay—in an endless mutually distrustful power struggle with your child. Second, giving some slack tonight doesn't mean that he will or won't spontaneously load the dishwasher tomorrow night.)

Whether it's a positive scene or a negative scene, this is the process of your both knowing where you stand with each other. It is precisely this that is the eight-hundred-pound elephant in the room, in families lacking a normal parent-child relationship.

When the scene is not positive, when a parent has reached the end of the rope, *this* is what is not addressed—that the relationship with her child and the chores is not one of mutual trust. Oh, everything else is addressed, the petty debating and arguing about why he needs to do the chore, how often he's done chores this week, how you never ask his siblings to do their chores, and how you'll threaten to toss his video game. But the *basis* for this wheel spinning is *never* discussed.

If you're reading this, you know how caught up you and your child get in this *other* agenda, the bitter control wrestling and power struggles occurring when your child refuses to do a chore. *You* want a remedy for this *now*.

And the remedy for this is to focus on where you both stand with each other. (No, the immediate remedy is *not* to see who does the chore.) If you've reached the end of *your* rope, you have *nothing* else to say except for this: "Tucker, you've proven your point. You can't trust my reasons for asking for your help. I can't trust you to help me out. This is where we stand with each other. This makes me feel sad, hurt, and let down. If you'd rather we trust each other, I'm willing to discuss it with you. But I'm done right now."

Then observe your son's decision to keep the mistrust going. For as long as he does this, you remove yourself from the emotional scene. You do not need more. He has proven to you where *he* stands. Your job at this point is *not* to try to wrestle things around because, by doing so, you'll show him that you **care so much** that he **doesn't need to care** about where the relationship stands.

> It is precisely your trying to wrestle things around that has brought you to this book!

But if your child refuses to do the chore and slips in the arrogant, disrespectful attitude, what exactly does your letting it go accomplish? I know you might be asking this right now. You think nothing's been accomplished. Dishes aren't getting done,

The Tyranny of Unconditional Love

and Tucker thinks he *won!* But ask yourself, "What exactly has he won?" His refusal to do the dishes—that is, the struggle over power that evening involving a chore—won out over your needing him to help you. He showed *you*, didn't he? You're standing in the kitchen watching him refuse to load the washer and watching him gloat perhaps?

The trick here is to detach from that power play. Unfold that emotional ten-foot pole. Watching him refuse to help you does *not* demand a move on your part, other than quiet observation. If you try to top him at that point, you're playing along with his agenda and *not* your parental agenda, which, remember, is to teach him how our world works and to teach him how his *refusal* would be received by another adult in our world. You, the parent, are there to show him the importance of mutual cooperation and respect. You're not there to "win" that power struggle. (And you can bet on it. Your not sparring with him will disappoint him.)

In the context of this book's major theme, he decided not to contribute to the household's work of the evening. *That* is what you respond to. You respond to him by letting him know that he let you down; you *don't* respond to him by letting him know that you're about to play his power game. If you play that game, you're not parenting him. If parenting is modeling the real world to your child, then do it. Your composure, your letting him know he let you down, and your silence thereafter will fulfill your role as a parent. Meeting his gaze with sadness and hurt in your eyes, with your body language suggesting disappointment and emotional withdrawal—this is your response.

You subtly withdraw yourself from him and from whatever it is he's won. Your not playing his game will teach him an important lesson: that his "win" or his victory is an empty one. It didn't win him a thing. What it *did* do is "win" your mistrust of him, your silence, and your emotional withdrawal. The rest of the evening, you're polite to him, you respond to things he says, or you help him with homework or whatever it is. But you do *not* show warmth, and you do not show any enjoyment in his company. With a distant look in your eyes, you seem preoccupied. You're not really engaged with him—because he let you down. You are no longer available to emotionally relate to him. You might be asking, "But what if he says nothing to me or he completely ignores me?" If he does *that*, well, you get a night off. I saw a mother and father who had come to the agreement to ground their two daughters when necessary. But it was usually the father who announced, "That's it. You're both grounded!" Their mother was left to feel that she had to, essentially, be available for them because they were grounded, which placed them at home and left to their own devices. They usually relied on her to provide some kind of activity or cure for their boredom. (Of course, if their mom gave in to her guilt feelings and eased their boredom, it would negate the negative intent of the grounding *and* it would serve to split mother off from father.)

When your child chooses to thwart you and not help with, say, the dirty dishes, his or her disrespect can chip away at your self-esteem and confidence as a parent. When you're standing there in the kitchen, watching her disappoint you, please do *not* focus on her not doing the *dishes*. Instead, please focus on her choice to not cooperate, not reciprocate, and not respect the relationship. *That* is what she chose to do. This choice will affect her sooner or later if she adopts a pattern of betraying and disrespecting others. Her "winning" the moment is not free, and it has a "price," which she will, inevitably, pay in the future if she does not pay it now.. (So why not get it over with, in the safety of your relationship?)

Your parent role demands that you show your child what will happen in life if she chooses to betray another's trust. The effectiveness of traffic lights, for example, depends on our internalized sense of obligation to obey them. If we did not internalize the need to obey them, we'd have police officers at every intersection. Our internalization of the goodness of obeying traffic lights indicates that we can be trusted. If I run through a red light, I am choosing to betray a trust. The police trust me to obey the light, and if I let them down, I will pay in the future. I carry forward my awareness of betraying that trust into an awareness that I will pay for it. THIS is your job of parenting your child. You teach her the awesome value of respecting a relationship and anticipating the effect her decisions will have on your future together. (Sometimes, as adults, we take things like this for granted. But we had to learn these life rules, didn't we? I suspect that, sometimes, we unwittingly make the assumption that our child already knows some of these principles before we've ever even broached the subject in our role as mentor.)

Crying

What do you hear, see, and feel when your child cries? It depends on his age and the circumstances, of course. What his crying *means* to you also depends on his age and the circumstances. But independent of age and circumstances, crying is an attention grabber. The reason for your child's getting your attention — starting much earlier in life than you think — depends enormously on your relationship with him.

You are conscientious. You bonded with your child during the crucial period of three months to eighteen months of age, and you did this by consistently responding to his needs. Being human, you weren't 100 percent consistent, and your child intuitively developed a grasp of your "style." How many minutes "late" would you be before bringing him your breast or bottle or changing his diaper? His bond with you incorporated a "wait" time during which he'd remind you — by crying or fussing — that you're late. This was a cry of *need*, reminding you of how utterly dependent he was on you.

As she nears the "terrible twos" and she's walking around showing interest in things, you've childproofed your home by putting shields on electrical outlets, for example. And so she begins incorporating your style of setting limits with her. Building her into a socially acceptable human being is a hard thing to do, but it is the essence of parenting. And your style will mirror your child's importance to you.

> Your child is so important to you that you will give her the information she needs about the world and how she must behave in order to be acceptable to our world.

By the time she's two or three years of age, the amount of trust established in your relationship will largely preempt her *need* to cry, and you intuit with anticipation your child's needs, and she knows that you'll be responsive. This is also true with cries of *fear*, as you can intuit what circumstances might instill a sense of insecurity in your child.

As she grows, she learns that her needs will be met and her fears stifled. You do not want her to presume that our world is contentious, that interpersonal interactions are inherently testy, conflict-ridden power struggles demanding a winner and a loser. Rather, you'd like her to develop an understanding of social limits and boundaries within which we cooperate with one another and value each other's feelings. These concepts are so important that nowadays we've stretched ourselves to the point where, in schools, "winners" and "losers" are labels to be avoided at all costs. Currently, some schools don't even keep the score of the baseball game or emphasize the importance of winning. Every child does "a good job, Buddy." I hear parents say that to their three-year-old simply for making it down the cereal aisle with only three demands. Holy cow! Suddenly every child is our buddy, and they all do good jobs. Is *every* child above average?

This is swinging the pendulum in the direction of praising mediocrity, in an effort to counter the increasing emphasis that is actually being placed on having an edge. (Look at steroid use in professional sports, for example.) As parents, we can prepare our children for this terrific ambivalence about succeeding, winning at the expense of others, and not being "a loser" by instilling in our children the value of a balance between healthy competition and mutual cooperation. Hence, your parent role also demands that you intuit when your child is crying for reasons other than fear or need or insecurity. You want to cooperate and wipe away tears of sadness, yet not give in to *tears of manipulation* in a contest of wills.

At this point, you might be reflecting on your own upbringing. Did your parents have this kind of "style," balancing competition with cooperation? (Ah. If they did, you probably wouldn't be reading this book, and you have no need for psychiatric intervention.) If they did not have this manner of representing the world to you as you navigated those formative years, you must—and this is a toughie—behave toward *your* child as if they did. Because remember, your job as a parent is nothing more than providing your child with a model of how our world works *at its best*. Think about baseball. Nine men get together and follow the rules of the game, each having a designated job on the team. The agenda is to cooperate with each other so as to maximize the chances of winning the game. So your job as a parent is to encourage your child to participate in your household as a member contributing to the well-being of your household (your world), so as to maximize the chances of getting through, say, the evening. Parallel to this is your responsibility to encourage her individualization and particular merits and talents.

Crying can have other meanings as well. During the terrible twos, your child's crying—more often than not—is a **cry of anger**. If you carefully listen to the sound she makes, you can tell the difference between a cry of need (or fear) and a cry of anger. There's nothing wrong with crying in anger. We do it all the time. Expressing anger through tears is good. But if you thwart your child's desire for candy at the Walmart checkout line, you know she's going to cry, correct? So what do you do about it? You've tried everything, I know. And she's not going to stop crying until you give in.

I know. Easier said than done. If you're reading this, you are truly at the end of your rope. I can't put it gently; you need to know that you are the creator of this mess. And the mess, as you know, is that he *knows* that you will give in to his crying. Somehow, you lumped angry crying in with cries of need and cries of fear. Not responding to his *cries of need* can make you feel inadequate. Have you allowed yourself to feel the same way with *cries of anger*? If so, this is the dance you both have been doing, perhaps for years, and your child has learned how to use crying to make you feel inadequate. *This is where you both stand in the relationship.* This is what you are choosing over the normal joy and happiness you deserve to have in the parent-child relationship.

> The longer you choose to delay parenting your child, the more frustration and insanity you are choosing for yourself in the future.

Your immediate situation with your child in the Walmart checkout aisle is the choice you have made over the years — not to parent your child, in this case giving in to cries of manipulation. The good news is that you still have parenting years left. You can now choose to parent your child and avoid more frustration and insanity in your future. The younger your child is, the easier this will be for you. Funny, though, you've heard this before, right? I'm writing nothing here that you don't already know. So why are you reading this?

You're reading this because all the times your daughter or your son has angrily cried in the checkout aisle, you thought you had to do something right away. Right then. Anything to shut him up and stop that awful wailing. End the scene and move on. And you continually find yourself in the same situation because — BECAUSE — you felt that you had to do something right then and there, and you did it. Your entire world focused on the need to stop that crying.

Excuse me? Is that right? As an intelligent person, you chose to engage with your child, essentially agreeing with your child, and you focused on that immediate situation. Period. I say this and put it this way because that is exactly what your child wants: to get you to lose sight of your job to teach him or her that it's not just the immediate thing at hand. Our world doesn't work that way. People register our behaviors as signposts telling them — and really, us too — where they stand with us. If you decide to pacify your child and she stops crying — which is really benefitting you and not her — and you then leave the store and drive home, you might enjoy momentary peace. *But* you also despair at having to dance around your child's tyranny. Your behavior, buying your daughter the sudden object of her whimsy in the checkout aisle, buys you a moment's peace. It buys your daughter much, much more than the trinket. Your behavior is a signpost telling your daughter where you stand with her. And at this point, it's screaming loud and clear, once again reinforced, that she is there to control you, and you are there to be kicked around, and, to boot, kicked around in front of others who might also feel the need for you to do something right then and there

Clowning Around.

But how *do* you handle the infamous scene at the store? I encourage you to focus on the important issues, which are the quality of your relationship with your child, where you stand with each other, and your parent job description. As you approach the store, think about and review prior episodes, because your first step in taking care of this situation is to take care of yourself by anticipating the event. Knowing your child as you do, be aware of how externally focused she is when bored. Boredom — anxiety when our expectations aren't being met — factors much more into these conflicts-waiting-to-happen than many people think. Now, if the job description of parent includes being an entertainer in public places, and if your child's locus of control is completely external to her, I suggest that you closely examine your qualifications as a professional entertainer — because little Amy might be so bored and so incapable of amusing herself that a professional clown, perhaps, might need to accompany you to the store...unless you have a few Oscars on your mantle, that is. Rather than wait for the bonfire to ignite and then feverishly scramble around — only to throw kerosene on it — take a private peek at your daughter's plight. She assumes that she needs an entire store to cure her boredom problem at that moment. If we recall the trust versus mistrust lesson we learned from Erikson, is it possible that you *never* dallied long enough to inject some frustration into your daughter so that she found her thumb to temporarily solve her own hunger problem while forced to wait an extra minute for nurturance? In other words, is Amy so regressed in her maturation that she lacks control over her own internal state, the moment you step into that store? If five-year-old Amy hasn't already begun to learn frustration and the need to tolerate some frustration by now, then that store's effective marketing strategies will hit pay dirt, and once the bonfire starts, you will focus on Amy's tantrum and the sudden need to put that fire out.

That's Amy's plight. Crossing over the store's threshold, she will become as young as an 18-month-old whose parents are continuing to unconditionally love her. She will suffer from the parent-child imbalance that's been bred into her for years. The intensity of her entertainment need is indirectly proportional to the amount of frustration you've already allowed her to experience, in other words, how much unconditional love you dared suspend in her growth and development to date.

If you recall Joey and his mother, Mrs. Enableson, in the principal's office with his outrageous behaviors and attitudes, please understand that the difference between him and Amy is a difference in degree and not a difference in kind. They both choose their attitudes and behaviors based on their meager knowledge of how the world works and what is expected of them. Joey's anger and entitlement barge ahead into violence; Amy's ignorance of frustration tolerance barges ahead into the store. They know not the priorities we place on appropriate expressions of anger and frustration, the torment their agendas cause their parents, the school, or the store, nor how embarrassing they are in their surroundings.

As you get deeper into the store, you're already armed with the expectation that Amy's need for boredom relief will engulf her, causing her to feel anxious, insecure, and frantic for an immediate cure. You have no clown, and your credentials as an

The Tyranny of Unconditional Love

entertainer are meager. The trap is set, so please don't be shocked. Don't be surprised at what you *know* will happen. (Taking the shock/surprise factor out will substantially reduce the emotional loading of this issue.) You've got enough to ponder without reacting as if Amy has the power to suddenly transform your shopping experience. Your priority is to get what you came to the store for in the first place and to minimize the scene about to unfold. Your guardian angel is neutrality, an indifferent, preoccupied demeanor reflecting nothing more than mild annoyance at the distraction Amy is providing. You are preoccupied with a big decision about when to start catching Amy up to reality. Certainly do not do it now, here, in the store, with no clown to help. And I advise you not to renew (or begin?) her education about the world's expectations when you get back home.

I strongly encourage you to wait for a neutral time when there's no strife, no urgent needs to quell boredom, and no power struggle. Put her education aside for now. And as the shopping trip unfolds, it is vital that you focus on the bigger picture. Your attitude, demeanor, comments, facial expressions, body language, and actions must convey to your child that you are registering something much more important than the immediate drama. If you choose to give in, you can and you must convey that you are actually focused on the nature of your relationship with your child *and your failing to reduce her ignorance about our world*. And you continue conveying this on the way home, later during dinner, that evening, and the next day. I tell you, do not focus on whether you're going to buy the toy or not. That's the smallest part of all this. Instead, focus on what your child says and does in the midst of your calm outward demeanor, because that will tell you volumes about the nature of your relationship.

Continue with a quiet composure until your son or your daughter understands. There's a quiet way about you—a calm, somber toning down of your expressions. You are preoccupied. There's a part of you that's not present in the room; part of you has gone away somewhere. Your polite attention to your child's needs and wants lacks emotional substance. Something is missing.

What's missing is the openness of your heart, your feelings sharply influenced by your guilt about letting Amy down. The parent-child imbalance caused her plight, and it's up to you to fix it. And unconditional love—a mix of pity for her mental illness, guilt feelings over finances, a conviction that you are mean, attempts to make something up to her, warmth, and acknowledgment of bits of goodness—is exactly the one thing that will *not* fix it. It will only make it worse. Have you ever inadvertently disappointed someone and then tried to make up for it? Has there been a time when that person kind of waved you off, indicating unreadiness to move on to your attempt to make amends? That's a cooling off period—a time to regroup and assimilate what transpired—that the other person needs before moving forward. It is a time when love—conditional or not—is just not in play. So removing yourself from being emotionally present for your child is the only thing to do. In other words, you are voided out.

> *You communicate that void to your child...*
> *and you'll find acquiring some leverage easier than you've ever imagined.*

"Okay, but what if this doesn't work?" you might ask. Then what? Well, the next time it happens, once you get home, it might be interesting to see if she remembers that you bought her magic boredom fix. Whether she does or not, once you're home, your agenda at that point is to leave the thing untouched and to return it to the store at your convenience. If she does recall your buying it, calmly and politely inform her that she does not have it to *keep*, because of the way in which she succeeded in getting it. *She didn't earn it.* She forced it. This moment, depending on how out of control your child is, can be mildly contentious or it can anger her so much that she might very well be physically aggressive. (In thirty years of doing this, only a handful of parents admitted that they'd

The Tyranny of Unconditional Love

seriously considered taking the item back to the store. In every case, they immediately dismissed the idea because they couldn't see themselves bothering to do that. They saw it as just another chore, another thing on their To Do list, completely overlooking the fact that it needed to be done in order to teach their child something very important. Instead, they focused on being inconvenienced.)

If you take this simple, common example of a child's tantrum literally forcing her parent to buy some unneeded trinket in a store, and if you explore its meaning, you might see that it symbolizes how you would not want your child to develop. In order to have gotten to that Walmart or Toys "R" Us moment, your relationship with your child is already a contentious, distrustful power struggle in which her agenda is how much she can get away with — often simply because of boredom and an external locus of control — and your agenda is to have some peace. The leverage is clearly on the child's side, with the parent *held hostage*. Unless some miraculous sudden chain of events distracts your child — heavily on the side of *your* external locus of control, because you have avoided parenting your child correctly — you're on pins and needles waiting for her to proclaim her "need" for a toy or something, very often not until the last minute in the checkout aisle. Her bored sense of entitlement prompts her to select something of "importance," and she demands that you buy it. Your negative, usually dismayed, response then triggers the conflict, and she won't stop escalating it because she really doesn't have to, and she knows it. She finally acquires the item through coercion.

Isn't this the same thing as acquiring something not earned? Theft, burglary, robbery, extortion, blackmail — these are synonymous, aren't they? By purchasing it, you've reinforced this idea, that your son can acquire things he hasn't earned. And it also teaches him that *you* will cure his boredom. Remember, your job of parenting is to teach and model the value of cooperation, mutual respect, and accountability. There's no free lunch. There's no unconditional love. Once you've bought that suddenly coveted toy for your overbearing child, if you do *not* take it back, you're reinforcing the notion that there is free lunch and that you do unconditionally love your child, leading him to assume that other people in our world will do likewise. (The logical next step, of course, is shoplifting. This inevitably leads to anguish for both of you, as you will both wonder whose fault it is. By the time he's sixteen or so, has he "chosen his own path and must now learn the hard way, on his own?" Or should you come to his rescue, bail him out of jail, pay his fines, and so forth? By seriously considering my approach to parenting, you have a better chance of avoiding that dilemma.)

In the next chapter, we take a look at what you can expect once your child realizes you're taking the unearned item back to the store. I can predict many of these things because the fact that you bought that item under those conditions speaks volumes about your disempowered relationship with your child. This relationship—no matter your child's chronological age—is between your playing the part of the incorrect adult model of our world and your child's playing the part of the two-year-old you suddenly find yourself dealing with.

CHAPTER 11

ACT YOUR AGE?

Erik Erikson considered consistent, reliable responsiveness by the primary caregiver to the infant's needs as crucial for the child to develop trust in her environment. As the infant progresses to the toddler stage, most mothers start to fudge a bit, increasing the time the child frets before they respond. This is good, because it introduces the child to a basic fact of our lives: frustration. The child's confusion about the longer wait time, say, for his bottle, might prompt a bit of thumb-sucking, which is actually a form of self-soothing in lieu of the bottle. This is good for developing self-sufficiency and an *internal* locus (place) of control. (*I* am responsible for how I feel, not you.)

The "terrible twos" is an unfortunate label. This stage of the child-parent relationship should not be "terrible." But the reality is that the child begins to mimic the parent's increasing use of the word "No." As the child experiences his mother persistently defying *his* desires, he then turns that around and starts defying *her* desires. Erikson's second stage, developing autonomy balanced with the structure of our reality—*Shouldn't I have some doubt about whether to exceed the speed limit?*—is a better conceptual framework for this stage of the child-parent relationship. Parenting will model the world's toleration of autonomy tempered with some doubt and thinking before one acts.

Calling a child "ornery" or "just being a kid" is a cop-out. When I hear, "Oh, he can be a handful," I cringe. You bring your oppositional, defiant, bullying, destructive child in to see me to medicate him, and you say with a smile (in front of him), "Oh, he's a handful all right!" What the hell kind of message are you giving the kid anyway? That smile, that euphemism—that is pure bullshit. But can I say that to you? Can I comment on your facial and body language that completely accepts the very behavior you describe as intolerable? Can I just for a moment get you to consider that medicating your child might *not* be the answer? Wouldn't you get up and leave, file a complaint, or see me in court? Wouldn't you, in effect, take your child's side here? Yes, many parents find my direct, to-the-jugular approach at least irritating, and at most appalling. For many reasons beyond the scope of this book, they somehow view their child's "orneriness" or "handfulness" as an expected part of childhood, not realizing that the initial "cute," pouty defiance their child begins to show around age two has completely gotten way out of hand. It's as if they are surprised that the child hasn't raised himself. What was once a cute, ornery, precious child, displaying healthy autonomy, initiative, and nonconformity—which are all normal aspects of psychosocial development—has incrementally stretched the bounds of this healthy development, creeping past the parents' awareness into this monster they can't control.

Without going beyond the scope of this book, we might consider Erikson's second developmental stage—autonomy versus doubt (ages two to four)—as most applicable to re-empowering ourselves as parents. The command, "Act your age!" addresses the emotional and behavioral regression we see in our children when they act autonomously *without doubting themselves*, wanting what they want when they want it and not taking no for an answer. Simply put, they regress to earlier ages in order to appear as if they are not able to comport themselves in ways acceptable and tolerable to the world. It's almost as if they're shouting, "I'm only four years old here. Gimme a break!"

Recently I saw a twelve-year-old girl with her stepmom. The family can't take it anymore. Darla is hateful, mean, and always cranky, and when she doesn't get her way, she says "hurtful, mean things," according to Helen, the stepmom. Plus, there are many times when Darla actually drops to the ground, shrieking and beating her heels into the floor, suspiciously picking bare floors in order to make the most racket.

"What do you say that hurts Helen's feelings?" I ask Darla.

Darla adopts an annoyed, puzzled facial expression, shrugs her shoulders, and mumbles, "I dunno." She then looks at Helen in a pleading sort of way, as if she's being tormented.

"Well, things...," Helen answers for her, following Darla's tacit prompt to come to her rescue. She glances at Darla, who is looking at her cell phone. "Can I tell him?" Helen softly asks her stepdaughter, who shrugs and looks quite pained and put out. Darla shakes her head and frowns, so confused and on the spot, my goodness. Darla is behaving like a pouty four-year-old right there in front of me, a pained look on her face. Gosh, it's almost as if I'm victimizing her with these questions. Didn't the three of us gather together today because of Darla's attitudes and behaviors? But now she winds up being the least verbal one in the room. (I wonder, if a child has so much to vent that she shrieks obscenities at home, is it *possible* to be this meek? This is her opportunity to speak her mind and appropriately air her complaints to an open audience—but not a peep.)

Helen looks at me angrily, demanding that we talk about bipolar disorder. Darla's mother, who left her seven years ago for another family, is bipolar, and Helen worries that Darla is, too. "We can't take it any longer. She says hateful, mean things!" Helen insists. It's obvious now that Helen is angry—with *me*! Darla, mute, is back to looking at her cell phone. She appears unable to express herself, totally evading the interview and skillfully guiding Helen to view me as *their* adversary. Darla then presses some buttons on the phone, her facial expression now pleasant, absorbed in her own world. Helen attempts to take the phone from her, but Darla resists, yanking it back and forth with Helen. It finally winds up in Helen's hand, but once Helen looks back at me, Darla grabs it back.

"And she's been saying these things for years?" I deliberately avoid the bipolar issue, trying to somehow make a point here.

"Yes. Couldn't you —"

"Well," I interrupt, "if she's been saying the same hurtful words for years, then I guess these words are no surprise anymore?" I press.

Helen then looks at me in shock. "Doctor, they are mean things to say! We just won't have that kind of talk in our house!" The implication here is that I am disappointing and enraging them because of my questions, rather than immediately recognizing that this is a problem only a psychiatrist can cure.

"And so you continue reacting to these things she says to you?" I meekly ask. (Meekly, because I'm going out on a limb Helen doesn't want to explore. Helen really doesn't want to do any work here, you see. And she certainly doesn't want to put any stress on Darla, who will likely get even worse because *she* is being asked to do some work here. Helen just wants an immediate fix. Darla couldn't care less.)

"Of course I react. Do *you* have a bipolar child, Doctor? Do you even *have* children, Doctor?"

Oh boy. The *Do you have children?* question. Helen is so defensive, she asks that rhetorical question to announce to me — and to Darla — that child-rearing is very difficult and that Helen is doing the best she can, bless her heart. This is very gratifying for Darla to hear because it reinforces the notion that Darla, especially with the language she uses (gasp!), is a pretty powerful person. But the process of the interview suggests the exact opposite: Darla is much too young and too frail and innocent to have to account for her attitude and language. She can hardly speak right now and is perhaps too young even to think.

But Helen is not just coming to Darla's rescue right then. She's being defensive mostly because she wants a medicinal fix for Darla's genetic illness. Period. She does *not* want to approach the dysfunctional family dynamics that are working to enable

Darla's attitude and behaviors. Helen didn't bring Darla to see me for an explanation of their interactions. *And* trying to explore how Darla's depression about her biological mom causes her the anger that she takes out on Helen introduces Helen's egotistical pattern of reacting to Darla's ploys. (To boot, Helen's haughty arrogance probably deserves some of Darla's anger.) This idea — family dynamics — means that Helen might need to look at her own issues. But all Helen wants to "work on" is Darla's bipolar disorder. (A more complete analysis reveals that Darla regressed to the age of three or four, which a Freudian would find quite convenient. Subconsciously, Darla seeks to recreate life *before her mom left her*.)

Many parents do not want to look at their own issues. Just like the mom who immediately dismisses the idea of taking the toy back to the store, because being inconvenienced preempts disciplining her child, we all shun the task of working on ourselves. It's not only inconvenient to physically return to the store — even at, uh, your convenience — but just imagine the scene once your child realizes that his easily won prize is being ripped away from him. You've already hidden the damn thing, because if you hadn't, he would have certainly tried to do something that would at least get it back into his possession, or at most make it nonreturnable. This confrontation could then involve either verbally or actually physically wrestling with him over this object. I highly recommend that you avoid a *physical* confrontation, because this will profoundly reinforce your child's thinking that a power struggle here is condoned, and, more importantly, it will display an inappropriately high level of caring about your child's issue — because physically attending to someone involves a great deal of emotional and physical energy. Therefore, you make sure the object is hidden. (Amazing, isn't it, that it's come to this? But please note that it's a statement about your relationship with your child. If it's gone this far, you *must* turn things around. And, also note that corporal punishment requires an amount of emotional overflow which is completely counterproductive with this approach to parenting. Remember, you're trying to remove yourself as causing or forcing your child to change his behavior, no longer interested in putting your ego on the line. You *do* care about his maturational conflicts, but you do *not* care about who should win the dispute.)

Ten-year-old Tommy shouts, "Where is it?"

You cringe. "Tommy, it's not here. You can't have it, because it belongs back at the store." (Notice that you don't say, "I'm returning it," because this introduces you into the consequence of his not earning it. Remember, you are observing the choice he made and are allowing the real-world consequence of his not earning it to happen to him.)

"What? But I want it! You're mean." He scowls at you. "You bitch!"

"Tommy, this is—"

"I WANT it now! Where is it? I want it! Bitch."

"It's not yours, Tom—"

"Oh yeah, says who?" And he proceeds to look for it, perhaps overturning furniture in his way. Depending on how disempowered you really are, this might get to the point of needing to call the police. And if it does, you can expect mayhem until they get there, as Tommy will do everything he can to make you pay for this and to make you suffer.

But if his tantrum doesn't get that far out of bounds, simply say, "Tom, you need to go to your room and cool off. We'll discuss this later."

"Bitch. You're so mean. You never get me anything!"

Now, at this point you must *not* respond by saying anything that defends your decision, like, "You already have one of those" or "We can't afford it" or "Didn't I buy you the Nikes you wanted yesterday?" or "I buy you everything you ask for!"

You must resist this temptation. You'd be surprised just how strong this temptation is. Most parents succumb to it in some way, but once you do succumb to this, you've allowed your child to change the subject from not getting something he didn't earn to a statement about your character as a mom and as a person.

Instead, you reply—and you *do* reply, because ignoring him will not work here—"Tom, you're absolutely right. This does seem mean to you, and I should stop getting you everything. Thank you for reminding me."

"Bitch! Bitch! BITCH!"

"Tom you're repeating yourself. Of course I can be bitchy." By replying to "bitch" like this, you've essentially told him that your self-esteem is not pinned to the current label he is applying to you. And you're also telling him that he might be more correct than he thinks. He might really have a bitch for a mom! *And* you're refusing to argue the point with him. Are you a bitch, or are you not a bitch? Do you buy him things or not, and so on. By avoiding the argument, you are removing yourself from the situation. This is *his* tantrum. Let him have it. Don't tantrum yourself back to see who can have the better tantrum.

At some point, he will leave the area. He's really been nasty to you. He *has* hurt your feelings, making you doubt yourself as a caring mom. It's your job at this point to let him know that he succeeded in hurting your feelings. You do this by erecting the emotional ten-foot pole around yourself for, oh, the next day or so, perhaps more. Whatever he approaches you with, and however he treats you after this hurtful tantrum, you react with the truth of what happened. He hurt you, he cursed you, and he defied and opposed you. He let you down. Your quiet, sad demeanor lets him know this. You are polite; you do whatever it is your parenting requires — setting the table, giving him dinner — but you're emotionally absent and preoccupied. It is your parenting job at this point to let him know that you don't trust him to cooperate or be civil with you, and you emotionally remove yourself, so that he doesn't have you to misuse anymore. You do not emotionally engage with him.

This is the most powerful leverage you own, the most salient message to him that giving people a problem will give *him* a problem. He will lose them for a while. They won't be around for him, and it will be very lonely for him, being ignored as an emotionally present person.

You've observed the choice he made. But what if there was a movie scheduled or some outing — something which you two would've enjoyed together? What then?

What then, indeed. I tell you to look at **that** as an opportunity to drive home your point. If Tommy saw the need to degrade you so much, to label you as mean and awful, why on earth would you then be worthy enough to enjoy something with him? He just got through making it clear he thinks you're a mean bitch. Well, okay. You don't argue with him. In fact, you can see his point. You can be bitchy; you can be mean. These things are in your repertoire, right? And so, if you're this terrible, why on earth would he find you worthy of spending time trying to enjoy a movie with you?

"Mom, uh, what about the movie? We're gonna go see the new *Harry Potter* tonight. You said…"

"I know I did, Tom." (You sigh. How can he suddenly flip like this? Three hours ago, you're a bitch; now you're supposed to enjoy a movie together?) "But I'm done now. The blowup that just occurred…I can't enjoy much of anything right now." (Note the change from "Tommy" to "Tom." Assuming his birth name is Thomas, this might seem picky, but it's more important than you'd think. "Tommy" is the diminutive of "Tom" or "Thomas." Sure, it's just a nickname, but it carries more weight than you realize in a situation like this. Calling him "Tommy" is addressing a younger version of "Tom," which might be a younger version of "Thomas." Whether you enjoy these detailed symbolisms or not, calling him "Tommy" is tacitly encouraging his regressed behavior here. I'm sure you've run across people who, in the fit of dispute, resort to the more mature version of their child's name. Some parents have this as an agreed signal between them and their child — that they really mean business now.)

"What? But you said, you promised! You're—"

"Please, Tom, before you call me 'mean' again…I know. I heard you. I'm mean. Promises should *not* be broken, right? You made your point. I'm beginning to understand now." (You can delete some of these words if you want. I include them to encompass your mental set at this point.)

No matter what he says or does after that — for the next few hours or days (how badly were your feelings hurt?) — you maintain your position. This mental set does include the concept of finally *respecting* what he said to you. By this I mean not disputing it, not defending it, not making excuses, but acknowledging that, like everyone else, he is capable of having a valid point. And you might even reflect with him, "Y'know, Tom, you've told me this so many times, I'm beginning to think you may have a point. Maybe you *do* have a bitch for a mother."

I saw a nine-year-old girl whose mom came up with an ingenious strategy, one designed to light a bulb in her daughter's head. Emma was always disappointing her mom, saying she'd clean her room and then not, promising to stay put after bedtime and then roaming the house, and so forth. One evening, after Mom removed Emma's dishes from the table—something she finally *accepted* that Emma would *not* do—she filled a bowl with Emma's favorite ice cream and placed it with a spoon in front of Emma. Emma loaded the spoon with ice cream and, as she placed it in her mouth, her mom took the bowl and upended it in the kitchen sink. Seeing Emma's huge eyes and gaping mouth, she said to Emma, "See, Emma, now YOU can't trust ME. How does it feel?"

This, as well as taking the toy back, illustrates for your child the concept of decisions having ripple effects. Mom had long ago stopped arguing with Emma about cleaning her room. It never got anywhere except to enrage both of them, and she'd wind up cleaning Emma's room anyway. So instead of allowing Emma to change the focus from mutual cooperation to mutual degradation, her mom merely observed the choices Emma made and then, in a *neutral moment* when neither one was upset, Mom turned the tables and responded in kind to her daughter.

See what this does and doesn't do? It does teach the consequences of our decisions and the value of mutual cooperation. There *is* something in it for Emma to clean her own room, and it has nothing to do with arguing with her mom. Cleaning up her room is not something she should do *for her mother*. This vignette does not act out a yelling match, seeing who is really right and who is really wrong regarding cleaning up Emma's room. This particular vignette also illustrates a parent refusing to treat her daughter like a fragile, blissfully unaware two-year-old. By showing that "what goes around comes around," Mom is giving Emma valuable information that specific behaviors *do* have lag times before consequences might occur. People do not forget how we treat them. And yes, Emma is old enough and capable enough to endure this awful letdown, seeing her ice cream fade from view.

Taking the toy back just might alert your child to the fact that just because he wins the fight in the store about getting or not getting a toy, it doesn't really win him a thing. The toy goes back. But much more important, it shows your son that you're not interested in winning a damn thing in the store. You're trying to teach him the value of earning something and not being given just anything he wants. If he didn't earn the toy, he simply doesn't get it. When you take the toy back, you've satisfied your job as a parent, teaching your son how our world really works.

I tell you again that settling in for yet another argument with your child about all the little and big things you dispute with him will not only get you nowhere, but it will reinforce your child's willingness to continue opposing and defying you. The very act of arguing satisfies his need for entertainment, for power, and for nurturance.

> It *entertains* because it's a challenge.
> It *empowers* because he knows
> he will ultimately win
> (you do unconditionally love him, right?).
> It soothes and *reassures* him that you
> care about and love him because of all the
> time and energy you're devoting to *him*!

There is no grace period during which your child has license to make life difficult for you. Being a parent is truly a 24/7 job. During the terrible twos, your child is testing you, trying to find the boundaries. Do you know that a baby is the most opportunistic of all humans? She gets away with everything—even shitting in public! And she has every right to do so. But with toddling, the child has the capacity to begin understanding limits. Her opportunistic delights run into the roadblocks of reality. Shoulds and shouldn'ts start appearing, ruining her license to act spontaneously at all times. Rather than focus on you or your child, think about the **relationship**; your child wants to continue being a baby. You need her to slowly stop being a baby. Your relationship with her is the key. Your relationship instills in her the idea of the limitations of our world. What is acceptable to our world? As autonomous agents, we have the privilege of acting autonomously, to take opportunities as they become available, but within limits.

If you had the opportunity to assault the jackass driving in front of you, would you take it? Would you be opportunistic in that situation? If you've been socialized correctly, you wouldn't. Ah, but would your decision to not make use of that opportunity depend on the presence or absence of a police officer? If it does, you have an external locus of control; the cop is preventing you from assaulting the jackass. If it doesn't, you have an *internal locus of control*; *you* are preventing you from assaulting the jackass.

You do not assault the jackass because you *doubt* whether you should or not, and you know that you'd feel ashamed and guilty if you did. You limit your own autonomy, which is the essence of this Eriksonian stage of development. Being "terrible" or "ornery" or "just a kid" has nothing to do with this stage or with your task of parenting your child at this stage.

I dwell on this stage of development because your child has repeatedly regressed to this stage of development, acting as if he or she were three or four years old. When confronted with this, you have perseverated—doing the same futile thing over and over—with your typical responses to suddenly having a two- or three- or four-year-old to deal with. It surprises you and catches you off guard, no matter how many times it's happened. I am asking you to stop, step back, anticipate, and for God's sake don't be surprised or shocked anymore. (You don't deserve that.) I am also asking you to finally—please, finally—*accept* the reality of what you already know about your child: she's not going to do her chores; he will curse you; she will sass you and ridicule you; he will slur your character and morals; and she will try to make you second-guess yourself and your motives.

> But now you have the tools and wisdom you need to stop this madness.

As a psychiatrist, I am here to evaluate your child and to advise whether medication is needed to help correct a chemical imbalance affecting her thoughts, motives, feelings, attitude, and behavior. In addition, I am here to evaluate whether a form of cognitive deficit—perhaps autism or mental retardation—contributes to her difficulties and might require psychotherapy or counseling in addition to medication. After this assessment, once the genetic, cognitive, or environmental trauma issues are acknowledged and targeted, I am here to help you understand that your relationship with your child might also need some help. The quality and nature of your relationship foreshadows your child's relationship with the world and with others in it. As a parent, you have the opportunity to give your child the tools she needs to negotiate effectively, positively, and happily with others.

Within the relationship you have with your child, you start to build the essence of mutual cooperation, which is the foundation of teaching your child what is acceptable, and you model it for and with your child. The nonsense about unconditional love might be largely semantic because, as we all know, unconditional positive acceptance of someone is, operationally speaking, actually highly conditional. That is, society accepts us on the condition that we fit. (It's called "goodness of fit.") The one who parents correctly wants his child to include societally-defined "good" behaviors and to exclude societally-defined "bad" behaviors. Fitting in well invariably means contributing to the mutually cooperative environment. The effective parent wants her child to grasp and then intuit the value of cooperating with others and to know when not to cooperate. Within this relationship, you and your child both evolve to **know** this. This leads to a mutually cooperative effort to make your household — your world — work.

Like, we're all in this together, this thing called Life.

Summary

> Ritalin fixes ADD.
> Abilify stabilizes bipolar disorder.
> Logically limiting your love
> leverages you
> into the meaningful, respected
> mom and dad
> your child absolutely needs for growth,
> development, and life — a life with
> minimal conflict and optimal fulfillment.
>
> I wish all the best for you
> and your children!

Your thoughts, sentiments, and feedback are important to me. I am interested in your experiences with this approach to your relationship with your children, and I welcome both negative and positive feedback along with your successes and frustrations with this method.

My email address is Paul@TyrannyofUnconditionalLove.net.

Made in the USA
Charleston, SC
23 April 2015